CONTENTS

Introduction 2

Validating Your Idea 28

Creating a Business Plan 48

Building a Prototype or MVP 69

Building a Strong Team 133

Adapting and Iterating Your Business Strategy 155

Managing Risks and Challenges 200

Maintaining Work-Life Balance 221

ZIED ILAHI

LAUNCH TO
LEGACY
A Comprehensive Guide to
Transforming Ideas into Thriving
Businesses

INTRODUCTION

What Makes a Dream Job Out of Your Day Job?
Many people seek more than simply a paycheck when looking for a happy and meaningful profession. They seek to make their daily grind a source of passion, meaning, and long-term impact. This chapter delves into the critical ingredients that can transform an ordinary day job into a dream job, one that not only pays the bills but also provides a sense of fulfillment and success.

1. Align with Passion and Purpose: To turn your day job into a dream job, align it with your passion and purpose. Consider what actually interests you, what you find meaningful, and how your skills may be used to support a cause or purpose that aligns with your beliefs. When your work is aligned with your passions, each task becomes a step toward a larger objective, making each day more rewarding.

2. Opportunities for Continuous Learning and Growth: A dream career should provide opportunities for ongoing development. Look for

employers or positions that promote professional development, offer opportunities to gain new skills, and support your personal and professional progress. The ability to broaden your knowledge and skill set not only improves job happiness but also positions you for future success.

3. Work Environment and Culture: A positive work environment can significantly impact job satisfaction. A dream job frequently features a positive and supportive work environment in which collaboration is encouraged and people feel respected. A caring workplace stimulates creativity, inventiveness, and a sense of belonging, transforming your day job from a source of revenue to a place where you may thrive.

4. Autonomy and Responsibility: Achieving autonomy and responsibility can elevate a monotonous job to a fulfilling profession. When you are given the opportunity to take ownership of projects, make decisions, and contribute to the organization's success, your work becomes more than just a list of responsibilities; it becomes a platform for demonstrating your abilities and making a real difference.

5. Recognition and Appreciation: Feeling valued and appreciated is crucial for job satisfaction. A dream job includes being recognized for your efforts and accomplishments. Knowing that your efforts are recognized, whether through praise, promotions, or other types of appreciation,

provides a sense of fulfillment that extends beyond the monetary components of the job.

6. Work-Life Balance: Achieving a healthy balance between work and personal life is essential for overall wellbeing. An ideal job supports a healthy work-life balance by allowing you to pursue personal hobbies, spend time with loved ones, and unwind. A job that respects and supports your personal life greatly improves your overall job happiness.

7. Financial Stability and Fair Compensation: An ideal career requires both passion and purpose, as well as fair compensation. Feeling secure about your financial status relieves stress and allows you to concentrate on your work without continual anxiety. Fair compensation acknowledges your abilities and efforts, instilling a sense of worth in your work.

8. Impact and Legacy: A dream career involves making a significant impact and leaving a lasting legacy. Whether you're developing new products, resolving important issues, or positively impacting others, knowing that your work matters and has an impact on the world gives a deep layer of meaning to your daily activities.

Following Your Intuition
In the enormous terrain of entrepreneurship, where plans and tactics frequently dominate the conversation, there is a subtle but powerful force

that may shape a company's destiny the founder's intuition. "Following Your Intuition" is more than just a chapter; it's a profound investigation of the art of listening to that inner voice that frequently whispers insights amidst the din of business problems.

The Unseen Advisor

Intuition, sometimes known as the sixth sense, is a hidden energy that inspires entrepreneurs to make judgments that defy logic and analysis. It's that gut feeling, that silent nudge, that drives visionaries to make decisions that appear crazy to the outside world. In "Launch to Legacy," we explore the concept of intuition as the unseen advisor, an ethereal presence that has played a critical role in the success stories of many renowned companies.

Developing Intuition in Entrepreneurship

Is it possible to cultivate intuition, or is it a natural skill that only a few people possess? This section delves into the different ways entrepreneurs can cultivate and grow their intuitive abilities. From mindfulness practices to promoting creativity, "Following Your Intuition" offers practical advice for building an atmosphere conducive to tapping into this intuitive reserve.

The Dance Between Risk and Intuition

Entrepreneurship requires risk-taking, and

following one's gut frequently means navigating unexplored waters. This part deftly weaves the dance of risk and intuition, showing how great entrepreneurs have welcomed uncertainty with open arms, guided by an intuitive compass that challenges conventional wisdom.

Learn from intuitive entrepreneurs.

Throughout history, some of the most successful entrepreneurs credit their success to trusting their instincts. "Following Your Intuition" methodically examines case studies of innovative leaders who embraced their instincts despite overwhelming difficulties. From Steve Jobs' bold product launches to Oprah Winfrey's savvy career decisions, these examples inspire ambitious entrepreneurs looking to harness the power of intuition.

Intuition and decision-making

Business choices are frequently accompanied by an overwhelming amount of facts and views. Here, we look at how intuition may be an important aspect of decision-making, offering a distinct perspective that complements the analytical method. "Launch to Legacy" illuminates the delicate balance between logic and intuition, demonstrating how combining these aspects can result in judgments that survive the test of time.

Navigating Challenges through Intuition

Entrepreneurial journeys are fraught with

difficulties, and it is during these turbulent times that intuition can prove to be a reliable ally. This part looks at how entrepreneurs may use their intuitive insights to navigate crises, pivot effectively, and turn misfortune into an opportunity.

Increased Mastery and Independence
In the dynamic landscape of entrepreneurship, the road from idea to profitable business necessitates constant growth and adaptability. "Increased Mastery and Independence" is a vital chapter in this comprehensive guide, offering light on the many factors that contribute to the transformation of fledgling ideas into enduring legacies.

1. Introducing the Path to Mastery:

Achieving mastery in any profession, including entrepreneurship, is a constant process. This section goes into the complexities of skill development, highlighting the value of gaining a thorough understanding of your business. From sharpening technical skills to mastering the art of leadership, "Increased Mastery and Independence" walks entrepreneurs through the steps required to advance their careers.

Entrepreneurial mastery involves more than just individual proficiency; it also entails cultivating a learning culture inside your firm. The section investigates ways to create a learning environment that encourages both personal and professional development among team members. By investing in ongoing education and skill development, entrepreneurs lay the groundwork for long-term success.

2. Exploring the Landscape of Independence:

Independence in business entails more than just financial autonomy; it also includes the ability to make strategic decisions, adapt to change, and carve out your own brand in the market. This section looks at the numerous aspects of independence, beginning with financial prudence and diversification.

Entrepreneurs frequently face the difficulty of reconciling autonomy with collaboration. "Increased Mastery and Independence" provides guidance on effective delegation, team development, and cultivating a trusting culture. It disrupts the delicate balance between micromanagement and empowering team members, allowing entrepreneurs to lead with confidence.

Furthermore, the path to independence entails harnessing technology and innovation. The section emphasizes the need to stay current on technological changes, embrace innovation, and adopt tools that improve operational efficiency. From optimizing procedures to implementing digital marketing techniques, entrepreneurs learn how to use technology to drive long-term development.

3. Establishing a Legacy Through Social Responsibility

True corporate independence goes beyond financial success to include a commitment to social responsibility. This section investigates the role of corporations in making a good contribution to society. It promotes ethical business practices, corporate social responsibility, and long-term efforts that benefit communities and the world as a whole.

By combining improved competence with a sense of duty, entrepreneurs can create legacies that go beyond earnings, making a lasting positive impact on the world. "Increased Mastery and Independence" guides entrepreneurs through the difficulties of business, resulting in not just effective leaders but also stewards of positive change.

Possibility of Finance
Navigating the financial landscape is possibly the most critical and challenging aspect of the entrepreneurial journey, from the birth of an idea to the establishment of a lasting legacy. The "Possibility of Finance" chapter is more than just a financial one; it is a dynamic investigation of

the lifeblood of any successful organization. In this section, we'll delve into the complex world of funding possibilities, strategic financial planning, and the symbiotic relationship between finance and innovation.

Unveiling the Financial Tapestry:

Understanding the myriad possibilities of money is like unraveling a rich tapestry of options, each one woven into the fabric of entrepreneurial success. Entrepreneurs have numerous options, ranging from traditional outlets such as bank loans and venture finance to modern crowdfunding sites and angel investors. We'll go over the advantages and downsides, explain the complexities, and guide you to the best financial fit for your venture.

Dancing with Risk and Return:

Finance is not a one-size-fits-all equation; it is a complex balance of risk and reward. Entrepreneurs must learn the art of risk management while taking measured risks to move their ideas forward. In "Launch to Legacy," we delve into the complexities of risk assessment, highlighting real-world instances of businesses that effectively exploited risk to achieve unprecedented success. Understanding the delicate dance between risk and return will enable you to make smart financial decisions that influence the future of your business.

Strategic Financial Planning:

A roadmap without financial guidance is like a ship without a compass. In this section, we walk you through the process of developing a strategic financial strategy that will not only sustain but also propel your organization to long-term success. From budgeting and forecasting to financial modeling, we provide a step-by-step guide to developing a financial plan that is aligned with your business goals. Strategic financial planning is the compass that guides you in the right direction, whether you're a startup looking for seed money or an established company looking to expand.

Navigating the Investment Landscape:

The modern entrepreneurial ecosystem is brimming with numerous investment opportunities, ranging from traditional sources to emergent trends. We delve into the complexities of managing this landscape, assisting you in understanding the expanding role of technology, shifting investor expectations, and disruptive forces that can redefine financial opportunities for your enterprise. Staying ahead of the curve allows your company to attract the right investments at the right moment.

Beyond Dollars: Creating Sustainable Ventures

The road from start to legacy is more than just money transactions; it is about creating long-term projects that go beyond monetary gain. This section delves into the concept of impact investment, examining how businesses might balance profitability and purpose. Understanding the growing relevance of social and environmental responsibility allows entrepreneurs to create a legacy that goes beyond financial measures, leaving a good impact on the world.

Individual Development and Progress

In the broad tapestry of enterprise, the thread of individual development and progress weaves an important tale. The road from inspiration to the realization of a profitable business is more than just a group effort; it is largely based on the personal development and improvement of the people driving the vision forward.

Nurturing the entrepreneurial spirit.
The entrepreneur's indomitable spirit is crucial to any successful venture. "Launch to Legacy" goes deeply into the complexities of cultivating this entrepreneurial spirit, examining the attitude, tenacity, and adaptability needed to traverse the tumultuous waters of business. Through enlightening anecdotes and real-world examples, we explain the route to self-discovery, encouraging aspiring business leaders to hone their particular abilities and use them to achieve their objectives.

The Power of Continuous Learning
In a world of constant change, the ability to adapt and evolve is critical to personal development. This section of the book expertly takes readers through the ever-changing landscape of knowledge acquisition. From accepting formal education to cultivating a culture of continuous learning inside one's entrepreneurial environment, "Launch to Legacy" emphasizes the need to remain knowledgeable, curious, and nimble in the face of changing circumstances.

Personal leadership and vision
A company is an extension of its leaders, and effective leadership starts with a clear and compelling vision. Here, we look at the complexities of creating and implementing a vision that not only drives personal growth but also serves as a guiding force for the entire organization. Readers will learn effective tactics for goal-setting, decision-making, and developing long-term leadership abilities.

Emotional intelligence and resilience
The entrepreneurial journey is full of ups and downs, successes and failures. To ride this rollercoaster, one needs to develop emotional intelligence and resilience. "Launch to Legacy" devotes significant focus to these critical components, providing practical insights into stress management, failure recovery, and establishing the emotional fortitude needed to

weather the storms of the business landscape.

Balancing work and life
In the quest for corporate success, it is all too easy to lose sight of the delicate balance between professional goals and personal well-being. This part tackles the critical requirement for a healthy work-life balance by providing solutions for time management, stress reduction, and developing meaningful interactions with loved ones. After all, long-term success is evaluated not only in terms of financial benefits but also in terms of improved quality of life.

cultivating a growth mindset.
A growth mentality fosters innovation and success. Through an investigation of psychological principles and case studies, "Launch to Legacy" provides the tools needed to create a mindset that sees problems as chances for progress. This section encourages readers to embrace change, learn from mistakes, and persevere in their pursuit of business goals.

Holistic Development: Mind, Body, and Soul
Recognizing the connection between mind, body, and spirit is critical in the business journey. Beyond the boardroom, "Launch to Legacy" promotes holistic development, recognizing the importance of physical health, emotional well-being, and spiritual fulfillment. A holistic approach to personal development includes strategies for maintaining a healthy lifestyle,

controlling stress, and finding purpose outside of business.

Harmony between work and life

Enhancing your work-life equilibrium is an additional advantage of transforming your regular job into your ideal career. It can be difficult to strike a balance between work and personal life in many traditional jobs because of their strict schedules and lack of flexibility. On the other hand, you can prioritize your personal obligations and create your own timetable when you are in charge of your own company or profession. You can engage in hobbies, spend more time with loved ones, and take better care of your physical and mental health thanks to this flexibility.

Creating an Impact

Ultimately, you can change the world by transforming your day job into your ideal career. You are more likely to provide goods or services that benefit other people when you are passionate about what you do. Whether you are resolving an issue, enhancing the lives of others, or supporting a cause you believe in, pursuing your dream career enables you to leave a lasting impression and significantly impact the lives of others.

In conclusion, creating a dream job out of your day job has many advantages, such as the chance to follow your passion, more control and autonomy, financial success, personal development, improved work-life balance, and the chance to change the world. Even if the path isn't always simple, the benefits are definitely worthwhile. Thus, if you have a dream career in mind, now is the time to start the process of making it a reality.

The Advantages of Launching Your Own Company

Choosing to launch your own company has the power to transform lives. It has several advantages that might improve both your personal and business lives. This section will discuss the many benefits of launching your own company and the reasons it's a worthwhile venture.

1.2.1 Achieving Financial Stability

A major advantage of launching your own company is that you can become financially independent. Being an entrepreneur gives you the chance to start a successful business that can bring you a sizable salary. Owning a business gives you the freedom to control your own financial future, unlike a standard-day job where your earnings are constrained by a set wage. You can benefit from your labor and accumulate riches over time by making the required sacrifices and showing your commitment.

1.2.2 Following Your Intuition

Establishing your own business allows you to follow your passion and make money off of it. It's possible that working for someone else prevents you from doing work that genuinely inspires and motivates you. As a business owner, you are free to select the sector and specialty that best suit your values and areas of interest. This enables you to discover fulfillment in your entrepreneurial path and wake up each day thrilled about the work you do.

1.2.3 Adaptability and a Balanced Work-Life

The flexibility that comes with starting your own business is another benefit. Being a business owner gives you the freedom to choose your own hours and terms of employment. As a result, you may design a better work-life balance that meets your priorities and unique demands. Owning a business gives you more control over your time and commitments, allowing you to travel, engage in hobbies, and spend more time with your family.

1.2.4 Development and Personal Growth

Creating your own company can be a life-changing event that results in substantial personal development. Being an entrepreneur comes with a lot of difficulties and roadblocks. You will be forced to step outside of your comfort zone by these challenges and learn new abilities, including leadership, problem-solving, and decision-making. You will develop important experience and become a more robust and flexible person as a result of starting and expanding your firm.

1.2.5 Liberty of the Arts

You may let your imagination run wild and realize your ideas when you launch your own company. Owning your own business gives you the freedom to develop and try new things, unlike working for someone else, where you could be constrained by rigid rules and procedures. You have the chance to invent a special good or service, come up with innovative marketing plans, and establish a brand that is a reflection of your goals and principles. When your ideas come to life, having this creative freedom may be immensely satisfying.

1.2.6 Stability and Job Security

In the quickly evolving job market of today, traditional employment is frequently unpredictable and unstable. On the other hand, launching your own company offers some stability and employment security. You are in charge of your company's growth and direction as its owner. You can reduce the risks brought on by shifts in the economy and the industry by diversifying your sources of income and keeping up with market developments. This sense of security can give you confidence in your ability to manage your career and peace of mind.

1.2.7 Bringing About Change

Making a difference in the world is possible when

you launch your own company. Whether it's by offering a useful good or service, generating employment for others, or contributing to charity causes, entrepreneurship enables you to make a significant impact on society. You may start a business that not only makes money but also improves the lives of others by integrating your principles and sense of social responsibility into your operations.

1.2.8 A feeling of accomplishment and contentment

And lastly, launching your own company can provide you with a tremendous sense of satisfaction and success. It is immensely satisfying to create something from scratch and watch it take off. Being an entrepreneur gives you the chance to build a company that will outlast you and leave a lasting legacy. There is no feeling like the satisfaction and pride you get from conquering obstacles, realizing your dreams, and building a profitable business.

To sum up, launching your own company has several advantages that can change your life. Enterprising offers a special chance for success and self-fulfillment, from flexibility and personal development to financial freedom and following your passion. By starting this path, you can build a company that will benefit the world and provide you with financial gains in addition to that.

1.3 Overcoming Typical Difficulties

It can be an exciting and fulfilling adventure to launch your own company and land your ideal career. It is not without difficulties, though. This section will look at some of the typical challenges faced by would-be business owners and offer solutions.

1.3.1 Anxiety About Failing

The fear of failing is one of the most frequent challenges that people have while launching their own company. Many people are paralyzed by their fear of failing or losing everything, which keeps them from taking the initial step toward their ideal career.

It's critical to change your perspective and see failure as a teaching opportunity rather than a setback if you want to get over this phobia. Recognize that every successful entrepreneur has experienced failure at some point in their career and that it is a normal part of the path. Accept failure as an opportunity to develop, learn, and enhance your company.

Additionally, surround yourself with a network of

supportive people who share your values and who can offer advice and assistance. Look for mentors or become a part of entrepreneurial networks so you can get knowledge from others who have conquered similar obstacles in the past.

1.3.2 Insufficient Resources

A typical barrier faced by would-be business owners is a lack of resources, including human, financial, and technological ones. In order for a firm to be successful, it needs funding, qualified staff, and the appropriate equipment and software.

This is a challenge that requires creativity and resourcefulness to tackle. Seek out alternate sources of funding, such as crowdsourcing websites, grants, and loans. While you're creating your ideal career, think about leveraging your own savings to bootstrap your company or making money from a side gig.

In terms of human resources, you should concentrate on assembling a solid team by hiring people who share your enthusiasm for your goals and objectives. To cut expenses, think about outsourcing some work or collaborating with independent contractors. Utilize technology to automate procedures and optimize workflows so that you can accomplish more with fewer resources.

1.3.3 Managing Your Time

Many entrepreneurs struggle with time management, particularly if they are trying to develop their dream business while also working a day job. It can be quite difficult to juggle the demands of a full-time job, personal obligations, and the duties of launching a business.

Establishing priorities and practicing efficient time management are essential to overcoming this challenge. Establish a timetable that enables you to allot time for every area of your life and set specific goals. Gain experience assigning assignments and outsourcing as required to save up time for other crucial pursuits.

Distractions should be avoided in order to concentrate on important tasks that will advance your company. To increase your efficiency and streamline your process, use productivity tools and strategies. To prevent burnout, don't forget to prioritize self-care and take pauses.

1.3.4 Insufficient experience or knowledge

A common challenge for would-be business owners is a lack of experience or knowledge in their target market. Because of this, navigating the difficulties of launching and maintaining a business may be difficult.

Spend some time studying and gaining the required abilities and knowledge in order to get over this challenge. Utilize industry events, workshops, and online courses to expand your knowledge and skill set. Look for mentors or advisors who can offer direction and assistance.

Building a network with experts in your field can also be very beneficial. Engage in online groups, attend conferences, and join trade associations to network with professionals and get insight from their experiences. To overcome this challenge, keep in mind that entrepreneurship is an ongoing learning process and that being flexible and willing to learn new things is essential.

1.3.5 Lack of Support Establishing a business can be isolating, particularly in the absence of a solid support network. Having no support from friends, family, or coworkers can make it hard to stay motivated and get things done.

Find others who share your entrepreneurial goals in order to get past this roadblock. To network with other entrepreneurs, go to meetups, join online communities, or join networking clubs. Remain in the company of like-minded individuals who share your objectives, as they can offer insightful counsel, motivation, and responsibility.

Talk about your goals and desires with your loved ones as well. Assist them in realizing the significance of your endeavor and the impact that their support can have. Inform them of the difficulties and benefits of being an entrepreneur, and include them in your path whenever you can.

Recall that conquering challenges is a crucial aspect of the business path. Through accepting challenges, looking for assistance, and always learning and adapting, you may get over typical roadblocks and make your ideal career a prosperous reality.

1.4 Establishing Reasonable Expectations

One of the most important steps to making your dream career a reality is to set reasonable expectations. While having lofty aspirations and great dreams is vital, it's also critical to keep your expectations grounded in reality. By establishing reasonable expectations, you can steer clear of needless disappointment and annoyance and concentrate on advancing steadily toward your objectives.

1.4.1 Being aware of the time and work needed

When setting reasonable expectations, one of the first things to take into account is the time and work needed to develop your idea into a profitable business. It takes time and effort to launch a business. Validating your idea, creating a business plan, building a prototype, obtaining capital, and launching your product or service all require time. It's critical to have a long-term perspective and realize that success won't come easily.

1.4.2 Controlling Expectations Regarding Money

Managing your financial expectations is another part of having reasonable expectations. Even if it is feasible to create a profitable company and earn a sizable income, it is crucial to realize that it could take some time to get there. You could have to use alternative funding sources or invest your own money in the first phases of your company. It's critical to be cognizant of your financial circumstances and ready to accept the risk that you may not turn a profit right away.

1.4.3 Seeing Failure as a Chance to Learn

Acknowledging that failure is a normal part of the business path is another aspect of setting reasonable expectations. Not every business will succeed, and not every idea will be a hit. It's critical to accept failure as a teaching tool and not allow it to demoralize you. Through establishing reasonable goals and acknowledging the potential for failure, you may confront obstacles with fortitude and gain knowledge from your errors.

1.4.4 Juggling Personal and Professional Life

It's easy to get carried away by the excitement of chasing your dream profession and giving your business all your attention. It's crucial to have reasonable expectations for work-life balance, though. Your general well-being and the success of your business may suffer if you burn out and neglect your personal life. For long-term success, self-care and setting boundaries are crucial.

1.4.5 Honoring Minor Victories

Setting reasonable goals and recognizing little victories along the way are equally crucial. Establishing a profitable company is a journey, and every step you take, no matter how small, should be recognized and celebrated. You may stay optimistic and motivated even in the face of adversity by acknowledging little victories.

1.4.6 Looking for assistance and advice
It is not necessary for you to handle everything by yourself when you have reasonable expectations. It can be really helpful to get advice and assistance from peers, mentors, or business coaches when navigating the difficulties of launching and expanding a company. Having a strong support system around you can provide you with the motivation and direction you need to stay on course and accomplish your objectives.

1.4.7 Modifying and tailoring
And last, having reasonable expectations implies being flexible enough to change course when necessary. The business environment is dynamic; therefore, it's critical to be adaptable and ready to change course when called for. You can overcome unforeseen obstacles and take advantage of new chances that present themselves by remaining flexible and open-minded.

To sum up, one of the most important steps in transforming your ideal work into a profitable business is setting reasonable expectations. You can position yourself for long-term success by realizing the time and effort needed, controlling your financial expectations, accepting failure as a teaching opportunity, juggling work and personal obligations, acknowledging small victories, asking for help and direction, and being willing to change and grow. Recall that creating a profitable company requires patience and effort, but you may achieve your ideal career with a strong will and reasonable goals.

VALIDATING YOUR IDEA

2.1 Determining a Need in the Market

Determine a market need before you start the

process of transforming your idea into a profitable company. Recognizing the market for your goods or services is the cornerstone around which your whole enterprise will be constructed. You may be sure that there is a sizable consumer base ready to pay for what you have to offer by determining a market need. We'll look at the measures you can take to find a market need and validate your idea in this part.

2.1.1 Market Research

Conducting in-depth market research is the first stage in determining a market requirement. To do this, you must compile data about your target market, rivals, and market trends. You can obtain insightful knowledge that will assist you in developing your business plan by having a thorough awareness of the state of the market.

Establish who your target audience is first. Who could be interested in purchasing your goods or services? What are their preferences, pain points, and demographics? Utilize focus groups, interviews, and surveys to acquire information and learn more about your target market.

Analyze your rivals after that. Who else provides comparable goods or services? What are their advantages and disadvantages? You might find market gaps that your distinctive solution can close by researching your competitors. Seek out chances to set yourself apart from the competition and offer value that they aren't currently offering.

Moreover, pay special attention to developments and trends in business. Exist any new technology or changes in consumer behavior that might have an effect on your company? To keep your product or service current and competitive, keep up with the most recent changes in your industry.

2.1.2 Determining the Pain Points of Customers

You need to be aware of your potential consumers' pain points in order to properly address a market demand. What issues do they have that your offering can help with? You may position your company as a solution provider and develop an appealing value offer by determining these pain spots.

Start by asking your target audience directly for input through surveys or customer interviews. Pose open-ended questions to entice people to talk about their difficulties and disappointments. Observe any reoccurring themes or trends in their answers. You may improve your product or service to better meet their needs with the use of these insights.

To find holes in the market, think about performing a competitive study as well. Are there any unmet demands or underserved client categories that your competitors are failing to address? You can adjust your product to close these gaps and increase your market share by recognizing these gaps.

2.1.3 Examining Your Concept

It's time to validate your idea after you have discovered client pain points and obtained information about your target market. This entails verifying that there is a market for your good or service and testing your hypotheses.

Piloting or beta-testing your idea is a useful method of idea validation. Get input on your product or service by presenting it to a select group of clients. This will assist you in improving your product as well as generate insightful case studies and testimonials that you can utilize in your marketing.

Another strategy is to gather potential consumers' email addresses and evaluate interest by setting up a landing page or pre-order campaign. Before devoting a substantial amount of time and money to the development of your product or service, you will be able to gauge the level of demand for it.

Additionally, think about asking mentors, advisors, or industry professionals for their advice and validation. Their knowledge and experience might offer insightful advice and assist you in further refining your concept.

2.1.4 Modifying Your Concept to Address Market Demands

It's critical to stay adaptable and receptive to criticism as you identify market needs and validate your proposal. Be ready to modify and refine your concept in light of the knowledge you gain from your investigation and testing.

Pay attention to what your customers have to say and consider their input. Are there any typical requests or suggestions that you could include in your offering? You may make sure that your offering consistently fulfills the changing needs of your target market by making improvements and refinements to it.

Recall that determining market demand is a continuous procedure. Remaining aware of your clients' wants and demands is crucial as your company expands and the industry evolves. By doing this, you may set up your company for long-term success and guarantee that your goods or services will continue to be in demand in a crowded market.

We'll talk more about the value of market research in the following part, so you may learn more about your competition and target market. You may improve your chances of success and build a strong foundation for your company by devoting time and energy to this important phase.

2.2 Carrying out Market Research

Performing comprehensive market research is essential before launching your own company. The process of obtaining and examining data on your target market, rivals, and market trends is known as market research. You will gain important insights from this research that will improve your decision-making and success rates.

2.2.1 Recognizing the Value of Market Research
Any successful firm is built on the foundation of market research. It enables you to comprehend the requirements and preferences of your clients. You can find market gaps, evaluate consumer demand for your good or service, and ascertain the viability of your business idea by carrying out market research.

Risk reduction is one of the main advantages of market research. You may recognize possible obstacles and create plans to overcome them by being aware of your target market and competition. Additionally, by using data-driven judgments rather than hunches or speculation, market research helps you make informed selections.

2.2.2 Clarifying Your Study Goals
Establishing your research objectives is crucial before you start any market research. What particular data are you trying to collect? Are you attempting to comprehend the characteristics, inclinations, or purchasing patterns of your target market? Which would you prefer—estimating the

market's size or locating possible rivals?

You can focus your efforts and make sure you get the most pertinent and helpful data by precisely establishing your research objectives. In the long term, this will save you time and money.

2.2.3 Research, Both Primary and Secondary
Primary and secondary research are the two primary categories of market research.

Gathering information directly from your target market is known as primary research. Surveys, interviews, focus groups, and observations can all be used for this. You can gain first-hand knowledge about your business and target market through primary research.

Conversely, secondary research entails obtaining pre-existing data. Industry reports, official publications, rival websites, and social media analytics are a few examples of this. You may learn a lot about market size, competitor analysis, and industry trends from secondary research.

To acquire a thorough grasp of your market, primary and secondary research are both crucial and have to be combined.

2.2.4 Data Collection via Interviews and Surveys
Interviews and surveys work well for gathering primary research data. Through online or in-person surveys, you can collect quantitative data from a sizable number of participants. Conversely,

interviews provide you access to qualitative data and enable more in-depth discussions with specific individuals.

It's critical to keep survey and interview questions focused, precise, and succinct. Make sure the questions are pertinent to your study objectives, and steer clear of leading ones. When collecting data, think about combining open-ended and closed-ended questions to get both quantitative and qualitative information.

2.2.5 Examining the Analysis of Competitors
One of the most important aspects of market research is competitor analysis. You can spot opportunities for difference and create a competitive edge by studying the plans, tactics, and capabilities of your rivals.

Begin by determining who your direct competitors are: companies that cater to the same target market and provide comparable goods or services. Examine their web presence, customer feedback, price, and marketing tactics. Look into areas of the market where your rivals are falling short and think of ways to bridge those gaps with your own special offering.

Analyzing indirect competitors—those who provide different approaches to the same issue—is also crucial. Understanding how clients currently resolve their issues will help you spot chances to present a superior or more creative solution.

2.2.6 Keeping abreast of industry trends

Since market research is a continuous process, it's critical to keep abreast of developments in the sector. Attend industry conferences and events, follow pertinent blogs and social media profiles, and subscribe to industry publications. You may see new trends, predict shifts in consumer preferences, and modify your company plan by remaining informed.

Recall that conducting market research is an ongoing endeavor. It needs to be a continuous process that guides your choices at every turn in your company's development.

In the next part, we'll talk about testing your ideas and getting input from prospective clients to help you solidify your business idea.

2.3 Examining Your Concept

The next stage in developing your idea into a profitable business is testing it after you have determined that there is a market need and have carried out in-depth market research. Before releasing your product or service onto the market, testing your concept can help you get insightful feedback that will help you make it even better. We will look at many approaches and techniques in this section to help you test your idea successfully.

2.3.1 Surveying the Market

Surveying the market is one of the most popular and efficient techniques to test your idea. Using surveys, you can learn about the requirements, preferences, and pain points of prospective clients. You may learn a lot about whether your idea is accepted by your target market and whether there is a need for your good or service by asking the appropriate questions.

It's crucial to have the following advice in mind when creating your market survey:

Identify who your target market is. Decide precisely which demographic you wish to study. This will enable you to better target your inquiries and guarantee that you are getting input from prospective clients.

Keep it brief. Short and easy-to-understand surveys increase the likelihood that respondents will fill them out. To avoid confusing respondents, avoid using technical phrases or jargon in your questions and stick to the topic.

Mix up the questions you ask: Use a combination of open-ended, multiple-choice, and rating scale questions to collect information that is both quantitative and qualitative. This will provide you with a deeper comprehension of the tastes and viewpoints of your target market.

Provide incentives: You might think about providing discounts, free samples, or entry into a prize drawing as a way to entice people to participate. By doing this, you may raise the response rate and get access to more data for analysis.

Analyze the data to find trends, patterns, and areas that need improvement after you have gathered the survey results. This will direct your next actions and assist you in making well-informed decisions about your product or service.

2.3.2 Holding Discussion Groups

Focus groups are a useful tool for evaluating your concept. Focus groups entail gathering a small group of people that resemble your target market to talk about and offer input on your proposal. Using an interactive method, you can get detailed insights, feedback, and ideas from prospective clients.

When planning a focus group, take into account the following advice:

Describe your goals: Give a clear description of the goals you have for the focus group meeting. Whether your goal is to get input on your product's features, price, or marketing messaging, having specific goals in mind will help direct the conversation and guarantee that you get the data you require.

Choose the appropriate participants: Select people who genuinely care about your product or service and who meet the requirements of your target market. To get a variety of viewpoints and thoughts, try to assemble a diverse group of people.

Make a conversation guide in advance: Create a list of inquiries and subjects to help direct the focus group conversation. This will guarantee that you cover all the relevant feedback topics and help keep the discussion on topic.

Encourage frank and transparent dialogue. Establish a welcoming and accepting atmosphere that encourages people to freely share their thoughts. Make sure everyone has a chance to voice their opinions and promote active involvement.

Assign someone to take thorough notes throughout the focus group session. This will assist in gathering all the important information and criticism for a subsequent study.

Examine the focus group notes after the meeting to find recurring themes, recommended changes, and areas that need work. Before continuing, use this input to improve your offering and make any required changes.

2.3.3 Performing Tests on Prototypes

It's critical to test your idea through prototyping in addition to focus groups and surveys for input. A prototype is an early iteration of your good or service that lets you test its overall usability, functionality, and user experience.

Take into account the following procedures when testing prototypes:

Describe the goals of your prototype: Clearly state your goals for the prototype testing process. Your testing process will be guided more easily if you have defined objectives, whether they be to test the overall user experience, find usability flaws, or collect input on particular features.

Build a prototype: Construct a model that closely reflects the finished good or service. Depending on your company's needs, this could be a digital mockup, a physical prototype, or a working prototype.

Determine who your intended audience is. Establish who the intended audience for the prototype testing is. This will assist you in finding people who meet the requirements of your target market.

Test the usability of your prototype by inviting people to interact with it and tracking their responses and behavior. Observe how simple it is for them to use the prototype, whether there are any obstacles or misunderstandings, and how satisfied they are with it all in general.

After every testing session, get participant input and make a note of any problems or ideas for improvement. Then, iterate. Make the required changes to your prototype based on user insights as you iterate and improve it using this feedback.

Prototype testing allows you to find usability problems or areas that need work ahead of time, which ultimately saves time and money. By refining your product or service based on actual user feedback, this iterative approach increases the likelihood that it will succeed when you introduce it to the market.

2.3.4 Examining Input and Making Modifications
It's critical to carefully consider the input you get during testing and to make the required changes to your proposal. Examine recurring themes, trends, and recommendations that show up in focus groups, surveys, and prototype testing. These comments will offer insightful information about what is doing well and what needs to be improved.

When you modify your concept, keep the following in mind:

Set priorities for feedback: Determine which comments are most important, then order the revisions according to their significance. Pay close attention to the problems that will most affect how well your product or service performs.

Iterate and improve: Make necessary changes to

your idea based on the feedback. To make sure you are headed in the right direction, make small adjustments based on user insights, and keep testing and getting feedback.

Remain faithful to your vision: It's critical to pay attention to criticism and make the required corrections, but it's also critical to remain faithful to your vision. Make sure that any modifications are in line with your company's overarching aims and objectives.

You may improve your idea and raise the likelihood that it will succeed in the market by testing it frequently, evaluating user input, and making necessary improvements. Testing gives you the chance to learn important lessons, spot possible problems, and make well-informed decisions that will ultimately support you in transforming your concept into a profitable company.

2.4 Examining the Rivals

It is essential to comprehend the competitive environment in which you will operate while launching a new company. You may spot possible risks and opportunities, learn about industry trends, and create plans to set your company apart from competitors by analyzing the competition.

This section will address the significance of conducting a thorough analysis of the competition and offer you doable guidelines for doing so.

2.4.1 Recognizing Rivals
Finding out who your rivals are is the first step in doing a competitive analysis. Direct or indirect competitors provide comparable or alternative goods and services. While indirect competitors could provide different goods or services but still meet the wants of the same clientele, direct competitors compete in the same market and aim to attract the same clientele.

Start by performing market research and compiling data on companies that provide comparable goods or services in order to discover your rivals. Online searches, trade publications, trade associations, and networking gatherings can all be used for this. List all of your rivals, including direct and indirect, together with their names, addresses, target markets, and main products or services.

2.4.2 Examining the Advantages and Disadvantages of Rivals
Analyzing your competitors' strengths and shortcomings comes next after you've discovered them. This study will show you how your company stacks up against the competition and point out areas where you can set yourself apart.

Start by looking at your competitors' main

advantages. Strong brand recognition, wide distribution networks, cutting-edge product offers, and a devoted customer base are a few examples of these. Gaining insight into the advantages of your rivals will help you pinpoint areas for development or new products.

Next, examine the shortcomings of your rivals. These could be areas of deficiency or underperformance, including inadequate customer support, a constrained selection of products, or antiquated technology. Finding these areas of weakness can enable you to obtain a competitive edge by providing a superior product or service.

2.4.3 Evaluating Positions in the Market

Market positioning is the process of determining how consumers view your company in comparison to your rivals. To find out how to set your company apart from the competition and draw clients, you must evaluate your market positioning.

Examine how your rivals are positioned first. Examine elements including their target market, price strategy, brand image, and USPs. This can assist you in determining any market gaps that you may take advantage of or places where your value offering can be more compelling.

Next, evaluate your own positioning in the market. Decide how you want customers to view your company and how you may set yourself apart from your competitors. This could entail focusing on a particular niche market, offering a distinctive product feature, or providing first-rate customer service. You may create methods to successfully express your distinct value proposition by analyzing your market positioning.

2.4.4 Tracking Rival Marketing Approaches
To remain competitive in the market, you must analyze the marketing tactics used by your rivals. You can learn more about their pricing plans, client involvement initiatives, and promotional methods by keeping an eye on their marketing endeavors.

Investigate the internet presence of your competition first. Examine their social media accounts, websites, and online marketing initiatives. Observe the language, imagery, and calls to action that they employ to draw clients. This can assist you in finding any weaknesses in their marketing plans that you can take advantage of.

Examine their pricing tactics next. Find out what your rivals charge for their goods and services, then contrast it with your own pricing plan. This will assist you in determining whether your pricing has to be adjusted in order to stay competitive, as well as how competitive it is.

Finally, keep an eye on the consumer engagement

initiatives of your rivals. Examine how they engage with their clientele via email marketing, social media, and loyalty schemes. This will help you find ways to enhance your own customer engagement initiatives and provide you with insights into their CRM tactics.

2.4.5 Making Your Company Stand Out

Creating strategies to set your company apart from competitors in the market is crucial, and it should be based on the insights gathered by studying the competition. By being different, you can draw clients who are searching for special value propositions and make an impression.

Determine your unique selling propositions first. These could include things like better customer service, quicker delivery, higher-quality products, or more user-friendly interfaces. Emphasize these distinguishing features in your promotional materials and proficiently convey them to your intended audience.

Next, concentrate on strengthening the areas where your rivals are lacking. Make sure you offer top-notch customer assistance if your rivals have subpar customer service. If their selection of products is small, think about increasing yours to meet the needs of a larger spectrum of clients. You can draw in clients who are unhappy with the products and services provided by your rivals by fixing these shortcomings.

Finally, keep an eye on the competitive environment at all times and modify your plans as necessary. It is imperative to be adaptable and up-to-date due to the swift changes in both market conditions and customer preferences. To stay ahead of the competition, always assess what your rivals are doing and modify your company plans accordingly.

In summary
One of the most important steps in transforming your idea into a profitable business is competition analysis. You can create strategies to stand out in the market and draw clients by analyzing the advantages and disadvantages of your competitors, evaluating your company's positioning in the market, keeping an eye on their marketing tactics, and differentiating your offerings. It is imperative to consistently assess the competitive landscape and modify your strategy accordingly to maintain an advantage in the dynamic business scene.

CREATING A BUSINESS PLAN

3.1 Establishing Your Goals and Vision
It is essential that you establish your vision and

goal before you start the process of transforming your idea into a profitable company. Your company's vision and mission statement will act as its compass, giving you direction and clarity as you confront the possibilities and difficulties that lie ahead.

3.1.1 A vision statement: what is it?

A vision statement is a succinct and motivational description of what you hope your company will achieve in the future. It illustrates your ultimate objective and the difference you wish to create in the world. Your vision statement should encapsulate the core goals and principles of your company and be both aspirational and grounded in reality.

Thinking deeply and reflecting are necessary when creating a captivating vision statement. To begin, pose the following queries to yourself:

What issue is your company trying to resolve?
What type of influence do you hope to have on society, business, or your clientele?
How do you see the long-term development and expansion of your company?
After you've responded to these questions, condense your ideas into a single, succinct sentence that captures your vision. Recall that an exciting and aspirational vision statement will inspire and motivate you and your team to work together toward a shared objective.

3.1.2 The Value of Having a Mission Statement

A mission statement describes the objectives and guiding principles that guide your daily operations, whereas a vision statement concentrates on the long-term goals of your company. It outlines the rationale behind your company's existence as well as the values that influence your choices.

Creating a mission statement entails knowing what your target market wants and needs, as well as coordinating your company's objectives with your personal beliefs. When creating your mission statement, think about the following inquiries:

What issue are you trying to solve for your target market, and who are they?

Which principles and values will guide your company's decisions?

How will your company set itself apart from rivals?

Make sure your mission statement is clear, memorable, and applicable. It should motivate your staff and clients while conveying the special value your company provides.

3.1.3 Harmonizing Your Goals with Your Mission

To develop a coherent and captivating story for your company, your vision and mission statements should complement one another and function in unison. Your goal describes the route to reach the destination, whereas your vision specifies the final destination.

Take into account the following to make sure your vision and mission are in sync:

Consistency: Your goal and vision should be in line with your own principles and convictions. They ought to demonstrate your ardor and dedication to your company.

Relevance: Your target audience should be able to relate to your vision and objectives. They ought to be in line with their goals and requirements, fostering a feeling of unity and purpose.

Clarity: Your staff and your consumers should be able to understand your vision and mission with ease. Steer clear of technical terms or jargon that could alienate or confuse your readers.

Flexibility: Your company's vision and mission statement should allow for both adaptation and flexibility, even as they serve as a framework. Your vision and goal may need to be modified as your company grows in order for them to remain relevant.

You lay the groundwork for the success of your company by clearly articulating your vision and goal. These declarations will direct your decision-making, motivate your staff, and draw clients who share your values. Spend some time creating vision and mission statements that are genuine and meaningful, then use them as a guide to help you on the thrilling path from concept to achievement.

3.2 Making SMART Objectives

An effective company strategy must have goal-setting at its core. It might be difficult to track progress and maintain focus on the tasks at hand without specific, quantifiable goals. This section will discuss the idea of SMART objectives and how you can use them to help your organization develop reasonable, attainable goals.

3.2.1 How Do SMART Goals Work?

The words "specific, measurable, achievable, relevant, and time-bound" are abbreviated as "SMART." With the help of this framework, you can develop goals in an organized manner and make sure they are specific and doable. Let's dissect each element of the SMART objectives:

Particular: You should have very clear and precise goals that do not allow for any opportunity for doubt. Rather than settling for a general objective like "increase sales," be more specific and state what you hope to accomplish, like "increase monthly sales by 20%."

Measurable: Having a mechanism to gauge your advancement toward your objectives is essential. Key performance indicators (KPIs) or specific metrics allow you to monitor your progress and make necessary modifications. If your objective is to "improve customer satisfaction," for instance, you might monitor survey results or customer feedback ratings to gauge your success.

Achievable: Although setting lofty objectives is important, they should also be reachable. When defining your goals, take into account your restrictions, abilities, and available resources. Impossible ambitions can cause demotivation and frustration. Make sure your objectives are difficult but doable.

Relevant: Your objectives should support your long-term vision and be in line with your broader business aims. Every objective needs to be well-defined and pertinent to the expansion and prosperity of your enterprise. Steer clear of objectives that have no bearing on one another or your overarching plan.

Time-bound: Giving yourself a deadline for your objectives makes them feel more urgent and keeps you motivated. Goals without a deadline risk becoming meaningless and undefined. Establishing a deadline fosters accountability and guarantees that progress is being made.

3.2.2 SMART Goal Examples

Let's look at a few examples to show how SMART goals can be used in many areas of your business:

Within six months, increase website traffic by 30%. This objective is time-bound (within six months), relevant (to generate more potential customers), measurable (by 30%), precise (to increase website traffic), and achievable.

By year's end, cut the customer churn rate by 15%. This goal is time-bound (by the end of the year), relevant (to enhance customer retention), measurable (by 15%), specific (lower customer turnover rate), and doable (by the end of the year).

Introduce a new range of products and make $100,000 in revenue in the first quarter. This objective is time-bound (during the first quarter), relevant (to expand product options), measurable (by the first quarter), achievable (based on market research and demand), and specific (start a new product line and generate $100,000 in sales).

Within the following three months, raise social media participation by 50%: This goal is relevant (to boost brand awareness and customer interaction), time-bound (in the next three months), precise (to increase social media engagement), measurable (by 50%), and doable (in the next three months).

3.2.3 Carrying Out SMART Objectives

It's time to incorporate SMART goals into your business planning process now that you are aware of their elements and have seen some instances. Here are some actions to get you going:

Determine your general business objectives. This is the first step in establishing SMART goals. What goals do you have, both short- and long-term? The process of defining goals will be guided by these objectives.

Divide your goals into particular ones: Take your company's objectives and divide them into manageable, targeted goals. Make sure every goal contributes to your overall objectives and meets the SMART criteria.

Establish benchmarks and measurements: Choose the KPIs or measures that will allow you to track your progress toward your objectives. Establish checkpoints along the route to monitor your progress and make changes as needed.

Assign duties: Clearly state who will be in charge of each objective, and make sure they have the tools and assistance they need to succeed. Assigning duties encourages accountability and guarantees that everyone is pursuing the same goals.

Review and modify your goals on a regular basis. Objectives shouldn't be inflexible. Evaluate your progress on a regular basis and adapt as necessary. If an objective is not being met, examine why it isn't happening and adjust as needed to improve the likelihood of success.

You may build a business roadmap and improve your chances of reaching your goals by putting SMART goals into practice. Because your company grows and new opportunities present themselves, don't forget to periodically assess and revise your goals.

We will go into creating a thorough marketing plan to advertise your company and successfully reach your target market in the following section.

3.3 Developing a Plan for Marketing

After your business idea has been verified and a strong business plan has been written, it's time to design a marketing strategy that will enable you to successfully reach your target market and advertise your good or service. Your company's success depends on having a well-thought-out marketing plan that will help you draw in clients, build brand recognition, and eventually boost revenue. In this part, we will go over the main processes for creating a marketing plan that complements your company's aims and objectives.

3.3.1 Determining Who Your Target Market Is
Finding your target market is a necessary first step in successfully marketing your good or service. The precise set of people who are most likely to be interested in and buy from your offering is

known as your target audience. You can effectively reach and resonate with your target audience by studying them and then customizing your marketing efforts accordingly.

Take into account these elements when determining who your target audience is:

Starting with their demographics, you should examine the age, gender, location, economic bracket, and profession of your possible clients. You can use this information to determine the target market for your product or service.

Psychographics: Examine the values, attitudes, interests, and lifestyle preferences of your target audience in greater detail. Having a deeper understanding of their interests and motives will help you craft marketing messages that truly connect with them.

Behavior: Examine the online activities, media consumption patterns, and shopping behaviors of your intended audience. You can use this information to identify the best marketing channels and strategies to connect with them.

You can better focus your marketing messages, select the most successful marketing platforms, and create tactics that will connect and engage your target audience if you have a thorough understanding of them.

3.3.2 Establishing a Logo

Developing a strong brand identity is essential to setting your company apart from the competition and fostering client loyalty. The visual components, message, and core values that characterize your company and shape the way your target market views it are all part of your brand identity. You may make an impression on the market that is distinct and memorable by building a strong brand identity.

Take into account the following actions to develop a strong brand identity:

Describe the values of your brand: Determine the core tenets and values that your company upholds. These principles will guide your decision-making and establish the character of your brand.

Create a voice for your brand by figuring out the communication style and tone that best represent your business's values and appeal to your target market. Across all marketing channels, your brand's voice should be the same, whether it's formal, informal, or funny.

Design a visual identity: By developing a logo, picking a color scheme, and selecting typography that captures the essence of your company, you may establish a visually appealing and unified brand identity. Maintaining consistency in your graphic aspects can help your consumers trust you and recognize your brand.

Create a brand narrative that effectively

conveys the mission, vision, and unique selling proposition of your company. Your brand narrative has to emotionally connect with and resonate with your target market.

Building a strong brand identity will help you stand out from the competition, foster customer loyalty, and make a lasting impression on the market.

3.3.3 Formulating a Plan for Marketing

Your precise plans and methods for promoting your product or service and accomplishing your marketing goals are laid out in a well-developed marketing plan. It guarantees that you maintain consistency and focus in your communications and marketing efforts by acting as a road map.

Take into account the following actions when creating your marketing strategy:

Establish definite marketing goals: Establish marketing goals that are SMART (specific, measurable, achievable, relevant, and time-bound) and in line with your overarching business objectives. For instance, during six months, your goal can be to raise brand recognition by 20%.

Select the appropriate channels for marketing. Determine which marketing avenues will help you reach your target most effectively. This could apply to both traditional and digital media, such as print, radio, and television advertising, as well as digital channels including social media, email, content, and search engine optimization (SEO).

Create marketing strategies: Choose the approaches you'll take to meet your marketing goals. For instance, content production, social media advertising, and influencer marketing could all be used to achieve your goal of raising brand recognition.

Make a marketing budget. Set aside money for your marketing initiatives, taking into account the expenses of every marketing channel and tactic. This will assist you in setting priorities for your marketing campaigns and guarantee efficient resource allocation.

Carry out and keep an eye on your marketing initiatives: Put your marketing plans and techniques into action while keeping a careful eye on their results. To maximize outcomes, evaluate important KPIs on a regular basis and modify your marketing strategy as necessary.

You can make sure that your marketing initiatives are strategic, focused, and in line with your company's objectives by creating a thorough marketing plan.

3.3.4 Using Channels for Offline and Online Marketing

It's critical to use a combination of offline and online marketing channels in order to reach your target demographic. Every channel presents different chances to interact with your viewers and advertise your goods or services. Utilizing many channels will enable you to reach and impact audiences as widely as possible.

Channels for internet marketing consist of:

Social media: To interact with your target audience, publish insightful material, and advertise your services, make use of well-known social media sites like Facebook, Instagram, Twitter, and LinkedIn.

The goal of content marketing is to inform and engage your audience by producing and disseminating high-quality information, including podcasts, infographics, videos, and blog articles. Content marketing fosters trust with your target audience and positions your company as a thought leader.

Improve your website and content for search engines to help it rank higher. This is known as search engine optimization, or SEO. By doing this, you'll raise your profile and attract natural visitors to your website.

Email marketing: To nurture leads, advertise your products, and foster client loyalty, create an email list and launch focused email campaigns.

Channels for offline marketing consist of:

Print advertising: To reach a wider audience, place ads in local periodicals, magazines, and newspapers.

Direct mail: To create leads or advertise special offers, send physical mailers or brochures to specific people or businesses.

Events and trade exhibitions: Take part in trade fairs and events tailored to your business to promote your goods and services, make new contacts, and increase brand awareness.

Public relations: Build connections with reporters and media organizations to obtain news coverage and provide favorable exposure for your company.

You can efficiently reach your target demographic and make the most of your marketing efforts by combining offline and online marketing platforms.

To sum up, creating a marketing plan is an essential first step toward realizing your business idea. You may successfully market your product or service and meet your business objectives by determining your target market, forging a distinctive brand identity, putting together a thorough marketing strategy, and leveraging a variety of online and offline marketing platforms. It is imperative to consistently assess and modify your marketing plan in light of industry developments, consumer input, and the results of your advertising campaigns.

3.4 Creating a Financial Plan

One of the most important steps in transforming your ideal profession into a profitable business is creating a financial strategy. A carefully considered financial plan will guide your decisions around pricing, profitability, and finance, in addition to assisting you in determining whether your business idea is financially viable. This section will go over the essential elements of a financial plan and provide you with helpful advice on building a strong foundation for your company.

3.4.1 Calculating Initial Expenses

It's important to project the initial expenditures needed to launch your firm before getting too technical with the finances. Everything from inventory and equipment to marketing and legal fees is included in the startup costs. You may establish a realistic launch schedule and ascertain the amount of money required by precisely projecting these expenditures.

Make a thorough inventory of all the costs you will need in order to determine your startup costs. To determine the typical price of each item, do some market research. It's important to be comprehensive and account for both one-time and continuing costs, such as rent and utilities, as well as equipment purchases. Remember to factor in any expert services you might require, including accounting or legal support.

After you've compiled a list of costs, give each item a price. When making estimates, exercise caution and think about including a contingency for unforeseen costs. Overestimating your expenses is preferable to underestimating them and then experiencing financial troubles.

3.4.2 Projections of Revenue

It's time to forecast your revenue after assessing your initial costs. Revenue predictions give you an idea of how much money your company will bring in over a given time frame, typically the first few years. Understanding the financial viability of your business idea and luring in possible lenders or investors depend heavily on these forecasts.

Estimating the size of your prospective client base and determining your target market are the first steps in creating revenue predictions. Next, figure out how many new clients you hope to bring on board in a specific amount of time and figure out the average revenue per client. When estimating, take into account variables like pricing, sales volume, and market trends.

It's critical to predict your revenue with realism

and caution. Refrain from overestimating your sales potential, as this may result in inflated hopes and unstable finances. Rather, concentrate on obtaining information and performing market research to back up your estimates.

3.4.3 Management of Cash Flow

One important component of financial planning is cash flow management. It entails keeping track of the money coming in and going out of your company to make sure you have enough to pay your bills and keep your cash flow positive. A positive cash flow is crucial to the long-term viability of your company since it indicates that you are bringing in more money than you are spending.

Making a cash flow projection is the first step towards managing your cash flow successfully. Based on your estimated revenue and expenses, a cash flow forecast projects your future cash inflows and outflows. It enables you to foresee any prospective cash problems and respond to them early on.

Keep a close eye on your cash flow and revise your projection as necessary. Determine whether there are any possible gaps in your cash flow and investigate ways to close them, including changing your prices, negotiating better terms with suppliers, or looking for other sources of finance.

3.4.4 Analysis of Profitability

Comprehending the profitability of your enterprise is important for formulating well-informed judgments and guaranteeing sustained prosperity. Analyzing your company's profitability means determining how profitable it can be by comparing its revenue to its expenses.

Compute your net profit margin and gross profit margin in order to assess profitability. The percentage of revenue left over after subtracting the cost of products sold is known as the gross profit margin. Conversely, the net profit margin represents the portion of income that remains after all costs, including interest, taxes, and operational expenses, have been subtracted.

You can find areas where you might need to raise pricing or cut expenses in order to increase profitability by looking at your profit margins. To obtain a thorough grasp of the financial health of your company, it's also critical to routinely analyze your financial accounts, including your income statement and balance sheet.

3.4.5 Sources of Funding

It's essential to look into funding options for your company after you have a firm grasp of your finances. Finance is essential, particularly in the beginning when you might not have made a lot of money yet.

There exist multiple funding alternatives, such as:

Self-funding is the process of financing a business with your own funds or assets.

Seeking financial assistance from loved ones who share your convictions about your business venture.

Bank loans: applying to a bank or other financial institution for a business loan.

Investors: drawing in money from those eager to provide capital in return for stock or a profit.

Crowdfunding: using internet platforms to collect money from a large number of donors.

Grants: Submitting grant applications to charitable groups or governmental bodies.

Every funding source has advantages and disadvantages, so it's critical to thoroughly weigh your options to see which one best suits your needs both financially and strategically. To make an informed choice, thoroughly investigate each alternative and, if needed, consult financial advisors or business mentors.

3.4.6 Reporting and Financial Controls

Establishing financial controls and reporting systems as soon as your company is up and operating is essential for keeping an eye on your financial performance and making sure that all legal and regulatory obligations are met.

Setting up rules and processes to efficiently monitor and manage your finances is part of implementing financial controls. This includes keeping correct and current financial records, putting internal controls in place to stop errors or fraud, and routinely balancing your accounts.

To monitor the financial performance of your company, you must implement strong reporting controls in addition to financial controls. To obtain insight into the financial health of your company, study and evaluate financial records on a regular basis. These reports include balance sheets, cash flow statements, and profit and loss statements. Utilize these reports to pinpoint areas in need of development, make wise choices, and update stakeholders on your financial performance.

In summary

One of the most important steps in transforming your ideal work into a profitable business is creating a financial strategy. You may create a strong basis for your company's financial performance by calculating initial costs, forecasting revenue, controlling cash flow, examining funding sources, and putting financial controls in place. Recall that financial planning is a continuous process, so as your company develops, make sure to periodically evaluate and revise your financial plan. You may overcome financial obstacles and realize your entrepreneurial goals more easily if you have a well-executed financial plan.

BUILDING A PROTOTYPE OR MVP

4.1 Realizing the Value of Prototyping

Creating a prototype, or minimal viable product, is an essential step in the process of transforming your idea into a profitable business (MVP). This section will walk you through the steps of designing and testing your prototype, as well as discuss the value of prototyping.

4.1.1: Describe a prototype.

Before devoting a substantial amount of time and money to full-scale development, you can test and validate your idea using a prototype, which is an early form of your product or service. It acts as a physical embodiment of your idea, allowing you to get input, spot possible problems, and make the required adjustments.

Depending on your business, prototyping might take many different shapes. It might be a straightforward sketch, a digital mock-up, or even a real model. The secret is to produce something that distills your concept to its core and enables you to obtain insightful information.

4.1.2 Prototyping's Advantages

The following are a few advantages of prototyping that can greatly influence your company's success:

1. Developing Your Idea

Making a prototype will help you see your concept come to life. Aspects that might not have been obvious during the conceptualization stage are frequently revealed by this method. It enables you to improve and rework your idea until it satisfies your target market's needs and is consistent with your vision.

2. Getting Input

Feedback from stakeholders, such as investors and prospective customers, can be obtained through a prototype. Their advice can assist you in determining opportunities for development, confirming your presumptions, and choosing the best course for your company. In order to properly tailor your product or service to the needs of your target market, this feedback is priceless.

3. Recognizing and Resolving Problems

A prototype can assist you in identifying potential problems or challenges early on through testing and user input. Early detection of these issues allows you to take appropriate action before devoting substantial resources to full-scale development. In the long term, this saves you money, time, and effort.

4. Bringing in Partners and Investors

A well-thought-out and useful prototype can be a very effective tool for luring partners and investors. It shows how dedicated you are to your concept and highlights its possibilities. Investors are more inclined to put money into a company that has a successful prototype and appears to have potential.

5. Developing self-belief

By testing and validating your idea through prototyping, you might gain the confidence to proceed with your business. It offers proof that your idea is workable and has a chance to be successful. When presenting your idea to potential partners, investors, and clients, this confidence is crucial.

4.1.3 The Method of Prototyping

Now that you know how important prototyping is, let's look at how to make a prototype for your company:

1. Establish your goals.

Prior to initiating the prototype process, it is imperative to establish your goals. With your prototype, what goals do you intend to accomplish? Are you trying to get customer feedback, test functionality, or present your idea to possible investors? Your prototype efforts will be guided, and you will be sure to concentrate on the most important components of your concept if your objectives are clearly defined.

2. Select the appropriate equipment and supplies.

Depending on your business, you must choose the appropriate materials and tools for your prototype. When creating a tangible object, materials like foam, cardboard, or 3D printing technology could be required. You can utilize design software, wireframing tools, or even make a clickable prototype for digital goods or services. Choosing your tools and materials should take your prototype's fidelity level, budget, and timetable into account.

3. Create a working model.
When your goals and resources are set, it's time to create your prototype. Start by using digital design software or paper to draw out your ideas. Concentrate on summarizing the essential attributes and qualities of your good or service. As you go, you'll be able to produce more intricate patterns and improve the prototype's appearance.

4. Construct your model.
Now that your design is complete, it's time to build your prototype. This could entail writing a digital interface, assembling physical components, or doing a combination of the two, depending on how difficult your idea is. Recall that the objective is not to produce a flawless final product but rather to develop a workable prototype of your idea.

5. Evaluate and rework
Testing your prototype thoroughly is essential once it is constructed. Get opinions from stakeholders, future users, and industry experts. Examine their suggestions and determine what needs to be improved. Utilize these comments to iterate through your prototype and make the required corrections and enhancements. Continue doing this until you are certain that your prototype satisfies the demands of your intended market.

4.1.4 Recap

An essential stage in taking an idea from conception to reality is prototyping. It enables you to improve your idea, get input, spot problems and fix them, draw in investors, and boost your company's confidence. You can produce a prototype that realizes your idea and lays the groundwork for a profitable business endeavor by adhering to the prototyping procedure described in this section. Recall that a thoroughly thought-out and tested prototype is an effective instrument that can advance your company.

4.2 Creating Your Model

After confirming your business concept and carrying out extensive market research, the next critical stage is to develop your prototype. A prototype is an early iteration of your good or service that enables you to test and improve your idea prior to devoting a substantial amount of time and money to full-scale manufacturing.

4.2.1 Clarifying Your Prototype's Goals

Clearly defining the objective of your prototype is crucial before you start the design process. Consider the precise features of your offering that you wish to assess and test. Are you trying to evaluate its appearance, usability, or functionality? Knowing your prototype's aims can help you make more informed design choices and guarantee that the final product successfully achieves your main goals.

4.2.2 Wireframing and Sketching

It's time to start wireframing and sketching your prototype once you have a clear idea of its function. Drawing basic, hand-drawn sketches of your product or service enables you to rapidly experiment with various design ideas and concepts. It's a low-fidelity method that concentrates on capturing your prototype's fundamental composition and structure.

On the other side, wireframing entails using specialist software or web tools to create more intricate digital representations of your prototype. It enables you to add particular features and functionality to your design in order to further develop it. Wireframes give you a visual depiction of the user interface in your prototype and assist you in seeing any possible usability problems early on.

4.2.3 Selecting the Appropriate Supplies and Equipment

Selecting appropriate materials and equipment that fit your budget and vision is crucial when designing your prototype. For low-fidelity prototypes, you might use conventional materials like paper, cardboard, or foam board, depending on the kind of product or service you are offering. These materials are affordable and enable rapid iterations.

You might think about utilizing 3D modeling tools and 3D printers to produce high-fidelity prototypes for more complicated designs. With the help of these technologies, you can create lifelike depictions of your product, making it possible to evaluate its form, fit, and function more precisely. But keep in mind that 3D printing can be pricey, so it's critical to balance the expenses and potential advantages.

4.2.4 Developing and Enhancing Your Model
Prototype design is an iterative process. It entails building several iterations of your prototype, putting them to the test, and analyzing the results to improve your design. You move closer to creating a final product that satisfies the demands and expectations of your target market with each iteration.

It's critical to get input from stakeholders, industry experts, and possible customers during the testing process. These comments will give you important information about the advantages and disadvantages of your prototype, enabling you to make wise design choices. Be receptive to helpful feedback and prepared to make the required adjustments to your prototype in order to make it better.

4.2.5 Working together with engineers and designers

Working with experts in design and engineering can significantly improve the quality of your prototype if you lack the requisite knowledge in these areas. While engineers can make sure your prototype is technically possible and complies with industry requirements, designers can assist you in creating visually beautiful and user-friendly prototypes.

Working with engineers and designers requires good communication. Make sure that everyone understands your vision, objectives, and requirements by communicating them clearly. Check and comment on their work on a regular basis to make sure the prototype meets your requirements.

4.2.6 Recording Your Design Process in Writing

You should keep a record of your decisions, iterations, and lessons learned during the design process. Not only can keeping a journal of your design process help you monitor your progress, but it will also be a useful tool for future reference. If you choose to pursue patents or other forms of intellectual property protection for your goods or services, it might also be advantageous.

To record your design process, think about starting a design journal or using project management software. Include wireframes, sketches, versions of your design, and any insights or criticism you receive along the way. This documentation will give you a thorough picture of your design journey in addition to keeping you organized.

4.2.7 Concluding the Prototype Phase

It's time to complete your prototype once you've iterated and improved it in response to user feedback and design enhancements. This entails developing a polished and useful version of your good or service that faithfully embodies your idea.

To make your idea a reality, you might need to work with manufacturers or production partners, depending on how intricate your prototype is. Collaborate closely with them to guarantee that your prototype is produced in accordance with your requirements and the necessary quality standards.

Recall that your prototype is merely a step toward the finished product. As you move through the development process, it's critical to continually assess and improve your prototype. Putting in the time and energy to create a well-thought-out prototype increases the likelihood that the final product or service will be a profitable venture.

4.3 Examining and Re-evaluating Your Best

It's time to test your prototype after you've designed it. One of the most important steps in the development process is testing and iterating your Minimum Viable Product (MVP). It enables you to obtain input, pinpoint opportunities for enhancement, and make required modifications prior to introducing your good or service to the public.

4.3.1 Specifying Your Approach to Testing

It's critical to establish your testing approach before you start testing your MVP. This entails choosing which features of your good or service to test, how to collect user input, and what performance indicators to employ. When formulating your testing plan, keep the following points in mind:

Testing Goals: Clearly state what you hope to achieve throughout this round of testing. Are you trying to find any technical flaws with your product, get feedback from users, or validate its functionality? You'll be able to concentrate your efforts and collect pertinent data if you know what your testing objectives are.

Testing Procedures: Select the techniques you'll employ to obtain input. User surveys, focus groups, interviews, and beta testing with a limited user base are a few examples of this. Take into account both qualitative and quantitative approaches to obtain a thorough grasp of the advantages and disadvantages of your product.

Testing Metrics: Choose the metrics that will be used to assess your MVP's performance. User engagement, conversion rates, customer satisfaction ratings, and any other pertinent metrics that are particular to your good or service can be examples of this. Establishing precise metrics will enable you to assess the testing phase's effectiveness.

4.3.2 Carrying Out User Testing

One of the most important steps in testing and improving your MVP is user testing. It entails getting input from your intended market to learn about their perceptions of your goods or services. Here are some guidelines for carrying out efficient user testing:

Determine Who Your Target Audience Is: Describe the traits of your target audience and seek out individuals who meet these needs. By doing this, you can be confident that you're getting input from the people who are most likely to use your service or product.

Construct Test Scenarios: Construct test scenarios that let users engage with your MVP in a realistic manner. These hypothetical situations need to represent typical use cases and assist you in assessing the functioning and usefulness of your product.

Observe and Collect Feedback: As participants engage with your MVP during the testing session, note their reactions and invite their input. Make notes about their experience, including any confusion, pain points, or ideas for enhancements.

Analyze and iterate: Examine the input you received from the testing session to find any recurring themes or problems. Utilize this input to fix any usability or functionality concerns found in your MVP and make the appropriate changes.

Iterating Your MVP 4.3.3
Iterating your MVP entails enhancing and fine-tuning it in response to input you have received from testers. The following are essential actions to successfully iterate your MVP:

Prioritize Feedback: Go over the comments you've gotten and rank the things that need to be fixed right away. To make sure that your product or service fulfills the demands and expectations of your target audience, concentrate on resolving the most important concerns first.

Make iterative changes: Based on the input you've received, make the appropriate adjustments to your MVP. This may entail enhancing functionality, introducing new features, or updating the user interface. Before proceeding, make sure you thoroughly test these modifications.

Test Again: Run further user tests to confirm that the modifications you have made are effective. This will assist you in making sure that the changes you have made have addressed the problems that have been found and have not created any new ones.

Iterate and test your MVP again until you are satisfied that it satisfies the requirements and expectations of your intended audience. You should get closer to a finished product that is prepared for release onto the market with each iteration.

4.3.4 Getting Stakeholder Input Feedback

Feedback from other stakeholders, such as investors, consultants, or industry experts, should be gathered in addition to user testing. Their observations can offer insightful viewpoints and assist you in further improving your MVP. Here are a few strategies for getting stakeholder input:

Pitch and Presentations: Use presentations or pitches to introduce stakeholders to your MVP. As a result, they will be able to evaluate your product or service and offer comments based on their knowledge and experience.

Meetings with Your Advisory Board: If you have one, set up frequent get-togethers to go over your MVP and get their input. Their observations might assist you in identifying blind spots and determining the best course for your company.

Attend conferences and events in your sector to network with professionals and possible investors. Take advantage of these chances to present your MVP and get input from experts in your industry.

Recall that stakeholder feedback can be just as insightful as user feedback. It can assist you in improving your MVP, matching your offering to consumer demands, and raising your chances of success.

In summary
An essential stage in developing your idea into a profitable business is testing and iterating on your MVP. You may improve your product or service and make sure it satisfies the needs and expectations of your target audience by establishing your testing strategy, carrying out user testing, iterating based on feedback, and obtaining insights from stakeholders. Accept the criticism you get and turn it into a chance to improve your MVP. You will get one step closer to landing your ideal job with each iteration.

4.4 Refining Your Product or Service

After creating a minimal viable product (MVP) or prototype, it's time to improve your offering to make sure it satisfies the demands and expectations of your target market. Through testing and feedback, this process includes making modifications and enhancements that ultimately increase the usability and value of your service. This section will discuss the value of improving your product or service and provide you with doable tactics to help you do it.

4.4.1 Obtaining and Examining Input

Feedback from your target market is one of the most important resources for improving your product or service. This input can originate from a number of places, including focus groups, customer surveys, and direct conversations with your clients. You may learn what features of your product or service are successful and what still needs work by proactively seeking out feedback.

It's critical to pose targeted questions that will yield useful information when obtaining feedback. Customers can be questioned about certain aspects they find helpful, any difficulties they have had, or their general level of happiness with your product. You can prioritize areas for improvement by identifying patterns and trends through the analysis of this feedback.

4.4.2 Reworking and Enhancing

It's time to iterate and enhance your product or service depending on the insights you have received after gathering feedback. In order to address the identified areas for improvement, this approach entails implementing small, gradual modifications and enhancements. You can continuously improve your offering and make sure it meets the changing demands and preferences of your target market by adopting an iterative strategy.

Prioritizing improvements according to their impact and viability is essential while iterating and improving your product or service. Begin by addressing the areas that require the greatest attention and proceed progressively down the list. This strategy enables you to efficiently manage resources and implement significant changes.

4.4.3 Improving the User Experience

Improving the customer experience is a crucial component of improving your product or service. The term "user experience" describes how satisfied users are with your service overall and how they engage with it. Enhancing the user experience can help you make a good first impression and win over loyal customers.

Take into account elements like usability, attractiveness, and ease of use to improve the user experience. To find any user-pain spots or areas of misunderstanding, do usability studies. Make the required changes to expedite the user journey and guarantee a flawless experience in light of the feedback that has been received.

4.4.4 Including User Feedback User feedback is a great way to improve your product or service. Engage your clients in conversation and take their recommendations and concepts into consideration while developing new products. This not only demonstrates your appreciation for their feedback but also aids in the development of a good or service that really fulfills their demands.

Think about putting in place a feedback loop where clients may offer recommendations or report problems. Examine and evaluate this input on a regular basis to find any repeating issues or common themes. By taking care of these issues, you can show that you are dedicated to making your customers happy and keep improving your product.

4.4.5 Quality Control and Testing
To guarantee the performance and dependability of your product or service, you must carry out extensive testing and quality assurance as you make improvements. Testing is the process

of methodically assessing your product to find any flaws, mistakes, or performance problems. Thorough testing allows you to find problems early on and fix them before they affect the user experience.

It is advisable to incorporate many testing methodologies, including functional, performance, and user acceptance testing. By using a thorough approach, you can make sure that your product or service satisfies the highest quality requirements and spot any possible problems.

4.4.6 Ongoing Enhancement

Your product or service will always need to be refined. You must never stop asking for input and making changes as your business grows and the needs of your target market shift. Encourage all team members to provide ideas and proposals for improvement by embracing an organizational culture that is focused on continual development.

To evaluate the effects of your improvements, monitor and analyze key performance indicators (KPIs) on a regular basis. To evaluate the success of your changes, keep an eye on user engagement, sales KPIs, and customer happiness. Utilize this information to guide upcoming revisions and guarantee that your product or service stays current and competitive.

You can keep ahead of the competition, satisfy

the changing needs of your target market, and provide outstanding value to your customers by consistently improving your product or service. Accept criticism, make changes, and refine your offering to produce a good or service that goes above and beyond customer expectations and propels your company forward.

Recall that there's no straight pathway from idea to success. It calls for flexibility, fortitude, and a dedication to ongoing development. You'll be one step closer to realizing your ideal career if you embrace the process of improving your goods or services.

Finding Funding

5.1 Starting Your Company From Scratch

The phrase "bootstrapping your business" refers to launching and expanding a company with little or no outside capital. It entails funding the operation and expansion of the firm with your own funds, such as credit card balances, personal savings, or earnings from the enterprise itself. Bootstrapping, which enables you to keep ownership and management of your company without depending on outside investors, can be a difficult but fruitful strategy. We will look at the advantages and tactics of bootstrapping your company in this part.

5.1.1 Advantages of Self-Staffling

There are a number of benefits to starting your business on your own that can help it succeed in the long run. The following are some of the main advantages:

1. Maintain ownership and control.

One way to keep complete control and ownership over your firm is to bootstrap it. This implies that you may manage your firm in line with your vision and that you are free to make decisions without interference from outside parties.

2. Develop your resourcefulness.

Being self-sufficient requires you to be inventive and imaginative while solving problems. When you're tight on cash, you'll develop your ability to prioritize, identify cheaper options, and make the most of what you have.

3. Pay attention to profitability.

Starting with an emphasis on profitability is encouraged by bootstrapping. Because you are using your own resources, you will have an incentive to make a profit and keep your firm viable.

4. Create a sturdy base.

You may create a solid foundation for your company by beginning small and expanding naturally. This entails building a strong clientele, improving your goods or services, and putting in place effective procedures and frameworks.

5.1.2 Bootstrapping Techniques
Strategic decision-making and meticulous preparation are necessary for bootstrapping. The following tactics will assist you in successfully bootstrapping your business:

1. Get Lean and Small-Started
It is crucial to start small and keep your costs down when bootstrapping. Pay attention to what matters most to your company, and cut back on frivolous spending. This could entail utilizing open-source software, working from home, or taking advantage of inexpensive marketing avenues.

2. Give revenue generation first priority.
When bootstrapping, generating revenue needs to be the first priority. Determine early on how to monetarily support your product or service and concentrate on attracting paying clients. This could entail providing incentives or discounts in order to draw in new clients and cultivate a devoted clientele.

3. Adopt a lean business strategy.
Using a lean business strategy can help you run your company more profitably and with fewer resources. This entails getting rid of clutter, streamlining procedures, and constantly enhancing your business. You can cut wasteful spending and increase production by being lean.

4. Make use of your network.

When bootstrapping, your network can be an invaluable asset. Speak with coworkers, acquaintances, and relatives who might be able to offer advice or support. They might become your first clients, lend their skills, or assist in promoting your company.

5. Look for strategic alliances.

When bootstrapping, working together with other companies or people can be advantageous to both parties. Seek out chances to establish strategic alliances that will allow you to pool resources, break into new markets, or take advantage of complementary skill sets.

6. Carefully reinvest profits

The growth of your firm depends on the prudent reinvestment of revenues once it begins to generate income. Give top priority to investments that will enhance your product or service or immediately lead to income growth. This could involve hiring important team members, developing new products, or launching marketing campaigns.

7. Remain flexible and adjust.

Adaptability and flexibility are necessary for bootstrapping. Remain receptive to criticism, keep an eye on industry developments, and be prepared to adjust your company plan as needed. Being adaptable allows you to take advantage of new chances and react quickly to changes.

5.1.3 Overcoming Obstacles

Starting a business on your own presents certain difficulties. The following are some typical obstacles you could encounter and methods to get beyond them:

1. Scarce Resources

A primary obstacle faced by bootstrapping is resource scarcity. To get around this, concentrate on making the most use of the resources at your disposal, give priority to necessities, and think of inventive ways to obtain extra resources, including trade deals or bartering.

2. Sluggish Development

When a company is bootstrapping, growth is frequently slower than when it receives outside capital. To overcome this obstacle, concentrate on creating a solid base, cultivating relationships with clients, and enhancing your offering on a constant basis. Long-term sustainability can be achieved through gradual growth.

3. The strain of finances

As the company owner, you may experience financial strain as a result of bootstrapping. Make a realistic budget, keep a tight eye on your financial flow, and look for ways to supplement your income with consulting or freelancing work. It's critical to keep personal and business finances in a healthy balance.

4. A small marketing budget

While it can be difficult, marketing on a tight budget is not unachievable. Make use of free or inexpensive marketing avenues, including content marketing, social media, and networking gatherings. Put your attention into connecting with and benefiting your target audience.

In summary

Starting a business on your own may be a fulfilling and inspiring experience. Through strategic ideas and the use of your own resources, you may create a profitable company while maintaining ownership and control. Even though bootstrapping has its share of difficulties, it also presents special chances for development, learning, and long-term sustainability. Always maintain your concentration, use your creativity, and adjust as circumstances change.

5.2 Looking for Capital

Getting financing to realize your dream job is the next step after developing a strong business plan and validating your business idea. One of the most popular methods used by entrepreneurs to finance their startups is to look for investors. Investors can give your company the money, know-how, and connections it needs to expand and thrive. This section will discuss the steps involved in finding investors as well as important things to remember.

5.2.1 Selecting the Appropriate Investors

Finding the correct investors for your business is essential before you even begin to look for others. Finding investors that share your vision and objectives is crucial because not all investors are created equal. When determining possible investors, take into account the following factors:

Experience in the Industry: Seek investors with a background in your sector or a similar subject. Along with money, they will also bring in important contacts and insights that can help your company.

investing stage: Various investors have specialized in various investing phases. While some choose more established enterprises, others concentrate on early-stage startups. Choose the stage at which your company is operating and seek out investors that share that interest.

Investment Amount: Take into account how much money you'll need and identify investors who can contribute that much. Make sure your fundraising requirements match the investment capability of your investors, as some have minimum and maximum investment thresholds.

Investor Network: Seek out investors who can assist your firm with their extensive network of contacts. An influential investor can expose you to partners, consumers, and other investors, all of which can be very beneficial to your company.

5.2.2 Establishing Connections with Investors
Developing a rapport with possible investors is an essential first step in getting company capital. Businesses that investors believe in and trust have a higher chance of attracting investment. Here are some methods for cultivating connections with investors:

Attend Networking Events: You can meet possible investors by going to industry conferences, startup pitch events, and networking gatherings. Have a succinct elevator pitch ready, and be ready to pitch your company.

Make the Most of Your Network: Reach out to people in your current network and request introductions to possible investors. Establishing personal ties is a great way to establish credibility and trust.

Participate on social media: on sites like LinkedIn and Twitter, follow and converse with investors. Contribute insightful content, leave thoughtful comments on their pieces, and position yourself as a thought leader in your field.

Seek Warm Introductions: Make an effort to obtain warm introductions from shared ties when contacting possible investors. Building trust and increasing the chance of a meeting are two benefits of a warm introduction.

5.2.3 Developing a Strong Pitch

You must create a compelling pitch that explains your company's value proposition to potential investors. The following advice can help you craft an effective pitch:

Keep It Brief: Because investors see a lot of pitches, make sure yours is brief and direct. Clearly state the issue your company addresses, the market opportunity, and your special solution.

Emphasize Traction: In your pitch, draw attention to any early traction you may have, such as collaborations, revenue, or customer validation. Investors are looking for proof that your company has what it takes to flourish.

Discuss the market potential: Clearly state the scale of the potential as well as the market requirements. Investors are looking to see evidence of a sizable demand for your goods or services.

Show Off Your Team's Strengths: People are just as important to investors as ideas. Emphasize the abilities and backgrounds of your team members and describe why they are qualified to carry out your business plan.

5.2.4 Bargaining for Investment Conditions

The next step is to negotiate investment terms with potential investors once you have captured their attention. This procedure entails figuring out how much your company is worth, how much stock you can give up, and the terms of the investment. When negotiating investment terms, keep the following points in mind:

Assessment: Ascertain the worth of your enterprise by considering variables including prospective market share, earnings, and anticipated expansion. Prepare yourself to defend your valuation to possible backers.

Stake in Equity: Choose the amount of equity you are ready to forfeit in return for the investment. Take into account the investor's contribution, the quantity of money you require, and the long-term effects of reducing your shareholding.

Specify the terms of the investment, such as the kind of investment (debt or equity), the timetable for repayment (if any), and any extra rights or responsibilities that the investor may have.

Legal assistance: To make sure that your interests are safeguarded and the terms are reasonable, it is recommended to have legal assistance while negotiating investment arrangements.

5.2.5 Expedient Research and Contract Sealing
Due diligence is the next stage after you and the investor have come to an agreement. The investor will carefully review every aspect of your company during this process, including the financials, contracts, and market potential. Be ready to respond to any queries or concerns that may come up and to provide the information that is required.

You can move on to closing the deal once you've finished your due diligence. This entails completing the paperwork, sending the money, and extending a formal invitation to the investor to join your company. Legal experts must be involved to guarantee that all required paperwork is in place and the transaction is completed without a hitch.

Recall that the process of looking for investors calls for endurance, readiness, and patience. To draw the proper investors for your firm, it is imperative that you conduct thorough research, cultivate connections, and create an engaging pitch. You may get the money you need to realize your dream career if you have the appropriate investors on board.

5.3 Loan and Grant Applications

You have a number of options when it comes to financing your company. Applying for grants and loans, in addition to bootstrapping and looking for investors, might be a practical approach to getting the money you need. Grants and loans can give you the money you need to launch or expand your company without requiring you to give up ownership or control.

5.3.1 Looking Up Grant Opportunities

Financial aid in the form of grants is non-repayable. Usually, government bodies, nonprofit institutions, and private foundations offer them. If you fulfill the requirements specified by the grant giver, grants might be an excellent source of cash for your company.

Investigate government agencies and organizations that provide grants in your sector or industry to start looking for grant opportunities. Seek out grants that complement your target market, mission, and business objectives. To make sure you meet all the requirements, it's crucial to carefully go over the eligibility conditions and application process for each grant opportunity.

Several typical grant kinds are as follows:

Grants for small businesses: These funds are intended especially to assist new and small enterprises. They can offer funds for a range of initiatives, including expansion, marketing, and research and development.

Research grants: You can be qualified for research grants if your company engages in creative research or development. These awards, which might aid in funding your research projects, are frequently offered by governmental organizations or academic institutions.

Grants for women- or minority-owned enterprises: There are funds available exclusively for women- or minority-owned businesses. These awards can offer financial assistance for a range of business needs while also promoting diversity and inclusion in entrepreneurship.

Non-profit grants: There are grants available only for non-profits, should your firm function as a non-profit organization. These awards might assist in paying for your projects, programs, and running costs.

It's crucial to closely adhere to the application requirements and submit all necessary supporting papers when applying for grants. Be ready to explain your objective, your business idea, and the difference you hope to make. Emphasize the intended use of the grant funds and how they complement the goals of the grant source.

5.3.2 Making Small Business Loan Applications
You can think about applying for a small business loan if grants aren't a good fit for your company or if you need more money than grants can offer. Typically, banks, credit unions, and other financial organizations offer small business loans. Grants are not repaid with interest over a predetermined period of time; loans are.

Determine how much capital you need and evaluate your financial needs before applying for a small business loan. Take into account things like startup expenditures, ongoing costs, advertising and marketing, and any other monetary requirements unique to your company.

You must submit a thorough company plan, financial accounts, and predictions, along with other pertinent documentation, when you apply for a small business loan. Your ability to repay the loan, business viability, and creditworthiness will all be assessed by the lender. A strong business plan and financial projections that show your company's potential for profitability and sustainability are essential.

There are several kinds of small company loans out there, such as:

Term loans: These loans offer a fixed amount of money with a fixed interest rate that is repaid over a predetermined period of time. Term loans are frequently utilized for certain goals, including refinancing existing debt, growing companies, or buying equipment.

SBA loans: To assist small firms, the U.S. Small Business Administration (SBA) provides a range of loan programs. Due to the SBA's 50% guarantee of SBA loans, lenders are exposed to less risk, and small firms find it simpler to obtain financing.

Credit line: A credit line is a flexible financing option that lets you take out loans up to a credit limit that has been set. You simply pay interest on the amount borrowed and can take out cash as needed. Credit lines are frequently utilized to control cash flow swings or meet short-term working capital requirements.

It's crucial to shop around and evaluate loan terms, interest rates, and repayment schedules from various lenders before applying for a small business loan. Think about collaborating with a consultant or financial advisor who can guide you through the loan application process and help you negotiate advantageous conditions.

5.3.3 Advice for Filing a Winning Grant or Loan Application

There are a few pointers that can improve your chances of approval when applying for a loan or grant:

Investigate and comprehend the requirements: Give each grant or loan opportunity careful consideration, making sure you are aware of the eligibility requirements, the application procedure, and the evaluation standards. Make sure your application is tailored to the goals and needs of the lender or grant source.

Create a compelling business plan. Applications for grants and loans require a well-written business plan. Your target market, competitive advantage, business idea, and financial predictions should all be stated in detail in your business plan. It ought to show the possibility of expansion and financial success.

Provide supporting documentation. Be ready to offer financial statements, tax returns, the resumes of important team members, and any other pertinent data that may bolster your application. Verify that all paperwork is correct, current, and well-organized.

Seek professional help if necessary. If you're not familiar with the procedure for applying for a grant or loan, you might want to think about getting help from a specialist. A business advisor, accountant, or lawyer with finance-securing expertise can offer direction and improve your prospects of success.

Maintain organization and follow up: To make sure your application is being considered, get in touch with the grant source or lender as soon as possible after submitting it. In order to maintain organization throughout the process, keep track of all correspondence, due dates, and specifications.

Recall that obtaining money via loans or grants may involve competition. It's critical to have patience, persevere, and be ready for any rejections. Make the most of any criticism or comments to strengthen your application for upcoming chances.

You can get the money you need to make your business idea a reality by applying for grants and loans. Spend some time learning about the several grant and loan options that are open to you, then create an application that is strong and showcases your company's potential. You can launch your firm into new markets and land your ideal career with the correct funding.

5.4   Alternative   Funding   Sources   and Crowdfunding

There are more choices available for financing your business than just the conventional approaches of taking out loans or looking for investors. Crowdfunding is a successful and well-liked substitute. With crowdfunding, you can raise money from a lot of individuals who are prepared to donate monetarily and who think your concept is great. This section will discuss crowdfunding and other alternative funding alternatives that can help you realize your career goals.

5.4.1 Crowdfunding: An Integrated Method

In recent years, crowdfunding has become increasingly popular due to websites such as Kickstarter, Indiegogo, and GoFundMe. These platforms give business owners a place to present their concepts and draw in possible investors eager to fund creative endeavors. There are a number of benefits to crowdfunding, including:

Access to Capital: By using crowdfunding, you can reach a large number of possible investors who might be considering your good or service. This can give you the money you need to start or grow your company.

Market Validation: Crowdfunding gives you the opportunity to test your ideas and determine market interest by putting them in front of a general audience. There is definitely a market for your goods or services if people are willing to invest in your enterprise.

Marketing and Exposure: Major media coverage is frequently attained by crowdfunding efforts, which can aid in increasing public knowledge of your company. Partnerships or media attention are among the other chances that may arise from this exposure.

To ensure the success of your crowdfunding campaign, make sure to adhere to these crucial steps:

Make an entertaining and persuasive pitch. Construct a pitch that effectively conveys the benefits of your good or service. To captivate potential backers, use storytelling techniques, films, and images.

Establish Achievable Funding Objectives: Ascertain the total amount of capital required to accomplish your company's goals. Give an explanation of the expenses and be open about how the money will be spent.

Provide attractive prizes: Provide prizes at several contribution levels to entice potential donors. These incentives may take the form of first dibs on your commodity or service, special goods, or unique experiences.

Promote Your Campaign: Use social media and your current network to get the word out about your campaign. To keep things moving forward, interact with possible backers, respond to their inquiries, and give frequent updates.

Keep Your Words: It's critical to keep your word to your supporters after your campaign has raised enough money. Give them their awards on schedule and keep them informed about your company's development.

Although crowdsourcing has the potential to be a successful financing source, it's crucial to remember that it needs to be well planned and carried out. Because every platform has different policies and costs, it's critical that you do your homework and fully comprehend the one you select. Moreover, success with crowdfunding is not assured, and standing out from the thousands of other projects competing for attention takes a great deal of work and strategic marketing.

5.4.2 Alternative Sources of Funding
You might look at other alternative funding sources in addition to crowdsourcing to support

your company. Among these choices are:

Small Business Grants: To assist small enterprises, numerous groups and governmental bodies provide grants. Non-repayable funding from these awards might be used for employing, expanding operations, or doing research and development, among other things. Look for grants that fit your company's objectives, then apply appropriately.

Business Incubators and Accelerators: Enrolling in a program can give you access to tools, coaching, and capital to help you expand your company. These programs can provide priceless help and direction, but they frequently have competitive application processes.

Microloans: Usually provided by community development financial institutions or nonprofit groups, microloans are tiny loans. The purpose of these loans is to assist business owners who might not be eligible for conventional bank loans. Microloans can be utilized for a number of business needs, including working capital, inventory, and equipment purchases.

Angel Investors: Angel investors are people who lend money to startups in exchange for shares of ownership or equity. These investors can offer essential advice and connections because they frequently have experience in the business. Making connections with possible angel investors can be facilitated by networking and going to industry events.

Peer-to-peer Lending: Peer-to-peer lending systems facilitate direct communication between borrowers and lenders. These online platforms act as intermediaries between borrowers and established financial institutions. Peer-to-peer lending is a viable substitute for conventional bank loans, possibly with more flexible terms and lower interest rates.

It's crucial to thoroughly assess the terms and circumstances of alternative funding choices as well as their possible effects on your organization. Choose the choice that best fits your business objectives and budgetary constraints because each has pros and cons of its own.

Recall that finance is but one component of the whole. Having a strong business plan, an appealing product or service, and a cleverly implemented marketing approach are all equally crucial. You may improve your chances of making your ideal work a successful reality by putting these components together.

Effective Marketing Strategies

6.1 Determining Who Your Target Market Is

Finding your target audience is one of the most important elements of creating a successful marketing strategy. The particular demographic that is most likely to be interested in and gain from your product or service is known as your target audience. You can effectively reach and engage with your target audience by knowing who they are and how to best target your marketing efforts accordingly.

6.1.1 Identifying Who Your Target Market Is

You must specify the traits and demographics of the individuals who are most likely to be interested in what you have to offer in order to identify your target audience. First, take into account the following elements:

Age, gender, locality, income, education, and occupation are all considered aspects of one's demographics. Knowing these demographic details will enable you to craft audience-relevant marketing messages that are specifically targeted.

The attitudes, interests, values, and lifestyle selections of your target audience are referred to as psychographics. It is possible to develop marketing efforts that specifically target their needs and desires by knowing their psychographics.

Conduct: Take into account the customs and actions of your intended audience. What kind of purchases do they make? How do they take in information? You can select the best marketing channels to approach them with by knowing their actions.

Pain Points: Determine the issues or difficulties that your intended audience is facing. Your marketing messaging can present your product or service as the necessary answer by addressing these pain points.

6.1.2 Researching the Market

It's crucial to carry out in-depth market research when you have a general notion of who your target audience is in order to confirm your assumptions and obtain more precise data. Obtaining information and insights about your target market, rivals, and market trends is known as market research. The following are some techniques for carrying out market research:

Online surveys can be used to collect thoughts and feedback from your intended audience. Inquire about their requirements, preferences, and difficulties in obtaining important information.

Interviews: Have one-on-one conversations with individuals in your target market to learn more about their driving forces, problems, and shopping habits.

Focus Groups: Set up focus groups with people who match the demographics of your target audience. Encourage conversation in order to get opinions and information about your goods or services.

Social Media Listening: Keep an eye on social media sites to see what people are saying about your sector, rivals, and associated subjects. This can give you important information about the requirements and tastes of your intended market.

Analyze your competitors' target markets, promotional plans, and USPs to gain insight into their business models. This might assist you in finding market gaps and setting your company apart.

6.1.3 Developing Personas for Buyers

You can develop buyer personas after your market research has yielded sufficient data. An imaginary depiction of your perfect client is called a buyer persona. It directs your marketing efforts and aids in gaining a deeper understanding of your target market. When developing customer personas, keep the following in mind:

Name and Background: Give your character a name and write a backstory that captures their characteristics, traits, and psychographics.

Objectives and Motivators: Determine your persona's objectives and driving forces. What do they hope to accomplish? What influences their decisions to buy?

Pain Points and Challenges: Recognize the

difficulties and problems that your persona encounters. What problems can your product or service solve?

Preferred Channels: Find out which channels your persona prefers for communication. Which do they prefer: traditional advertising, email, or social media?

Decision-Makers and Influencers: Determine who makes decisions and who has influence in your persona's life. When it comes to making purchases, who do people turn to for guidance and trust?

You may personalize your marketing messages, content, and advertising campaigns to connect with your target audience on a personal level by developing thorough buyer personas.

6.1.4 Honing in on Your Ideal Clientele

Your target audience needs to be reviewed and refined on a regular basis as your firm develops and expands. It is imperative to remain informed, as market trends, client preferences, and industry dynamics are subject to change over time. The following tactics can help you narrow down your target market:

Analyze Data: To learn more about the tastes and actions of your audience, regularly examine data from your marketing efforts, website analytics, and customer feedback.

Keep Up with Industry Trends: Stay informed on changes and trends in the industry that could affect your target market. This will enable you to modify your marketing plans as necessary.

Ask for customer input: In order to understand your customers' changing wants and preferences, ask for input from them on a regular basis. You can use this to better target customers and customize your products.

Test and iterate: See what works best for your target audience by experimenting with various marketing messages, mediums, and tactics. Utilize A/B testing and collect input to improve your strategy.

Recall that determining who your target market is requires constant effort. To make sure your marketing efforts continue to be successful, be willing to refine and modify your target audience as you obtain additional insights and data.

In summary
The first step in creating a successful marketing plan is determining who your target market is. You may develop marketing strategies and communications that are specifically targeted to your target audience by knowing their psychographics, behaviors, and pain areas. Maintaining a relationship with your customers and fostering business success may be achieved through carrying out market research, developing

buyer personas, and iteratively honing your target audience.

6.2 Establishing a Personal Brand

Establishing a powerful brand identity is essential to your company's success. Your brand is the impression that consumers have of your company, not just your name or emblem. It stands for the principles, character, and promise of your business. A strong brand identity may help you stand out from the competition, gain the trust of consumers, and develop a devoted following of clients. This part will go over the essential components of developing a brand identity and how to market your company to your target market.

6.2.1 Establishing Your Brand's Character

Prior to developing a brand identity, you must have a firm grasp of your company's mission and values. Establish your brand's beliefs, vision, and mission first. What is your company's mission? What goals do you have in mind? Which morals would you like to live by? You can build your brand identity's foundation by answering these questions.

Next, decide who your target market is. Who are the perfect clients for you? What are their wants, requirements, and areas of discomfort? Knowing who your target market is will help you craft positioning and messaging for your brand that will appeal to them.

It's time to establish your brand identity after you have a firm grasp on your industry and target market. Consider the perception you want people to have of your brand. Is it lighthearted and enjoyable, or somber and expert? Is it classic and dependable, or is it cutting-edge and innovative? Your brand identity should set you apart from the competition and appeal to your target market.

6.2.2 Establishing a Visual Brand

The visual representation of your brand is one of the most crucial components of brand identification. This covers your typeface, color scheme, logo, and general design style. All of your online presence—from your website and social media accounts to your packaging and promotional materials—should have a unified visual design.

Think about the message and the feelings you wish to arouse when creating your logo. Select hues that appeal to your target market and fit with the personality of your brand. Choose typefaces that convey the spirit of your brand while remaining readable. Your brand's visual components have to complement one another to produce a unified and enduring brand identity.

6.2.3 Developing Your Brand's Communication
Your brand messaging is just as important in conveying your brand identity as the visual components. Your tagline, brand narrative, and core themes are all part of your brand messaging. It should make it obvious what your company does, why it exists, and how it helps clients.

Create a catchy phrase that encapsulates your brand and appeals to your intended market. Your brand narrative should convey the background, core principles, and USP of your company. To captivate your audience and establish an emotional bond, use narrative strategies.

Your primary message ought to draw attention to the salient advantages and characteristics of your offering. They must be succinct, understandable, and captivating. Make use of terminology that targets and speaks to your target audience's problems.

6.2.4 Brand Guidelines and Consistency
When it comes to brand identification, consistency is essential. Make sure that your brand identity is applied uniformly to all online and offline touchpoints. Your website, social media accounts, packaging, marketing materials, and consumer interactions all fall into this category.

Create brand standards that specify how your logo, colors, typefaces, and other visual components should be used. Whether it's a third-party vendor or an employee, following these principles will guarantee that all representations of your brand are consistent in both design and message.

As your company grows, examine and update your brand guidelines on a regular basis. This will support your continued relevance and guarantee that your brand identity is coherent and in line with your corporate objectives.

6.2.5 Increasing Recognition of Brands
Building brand recognition is the next step after creating your brand identity. This entails developing an all-encompassing marketing plan that makes use of physical and online media.

Use social media channels to interact with your target market and tell the story of your company. Provide insightful, entertaining, or inspirational content for your audience. To increase your reach, team up with industry insiders or influencers.

Offline, think about taking part in trade exhibits, industry gatherings, or neighborhood projects. Collaborations, alliances, and sponsorships can all aid in raising brand awareness.

Analyze your brand awareness campaigns with indicators like website traffic, social media engagement, and client reviews. Make constant improvements to your marketing plan to increase brand awareness and audience.

It is possible to set your company apart from the competition, gain their trust, and develop a devoted clientele by developing a strong brand identity and expressing it to your target market. If you put in the time and effort to create a strong brand identity, your company will benefit greatly and be well-positioned for long-term success.

Recall that your brand is the opinion that consumers have of your company, not just your name or emblem. Verify that the way others perceive you is consistent with your mission, beliefs, and the promises you make to your clients.

6.3 Developing a Marketing Plan

Having established your brand identity and target market, the next step is to draft a thorough marketing strategy. A marketing plan is a tactical document that lists your objectives for marketing as well as the approaches you'll take to reach them. It keeps you organized and focused while acting as a road map for your marketing initiatives.

6.3.1 Identifying Marketing Objectives

Establishing specific, quantifiable marketing objectives is the first stage in creating a marketing plan. These objectives should be SMART (specific, measurable, achievable, relevant, and time-bound) and should be in line with your overall business goals. Your marketing objectives can, for instance, be to raise sales, generate leads, increase website traffic, or raise brand awareness.

Take into account the following while creating marketing objectives:

Who is your target audience, and what is the purpose of your marketing campaigns? Determine the demographics, psychographics, and behavior of your target market.

KPIs, or key performance indicators, are: Which measures are you going to employ to assess the effectiveness of your marketing campaigns? KPIs include things like website traffic, conversion rate, social media interaction, and the cost of acquiring new customers.

Timeline: What date do you want to reach your marketing objectives? Establish clear due dates for every objective to foster a sense of responsibility and urgency.

Budget: What is the maximum amount of money you are willing to spend on your marketing initiatives? Give top priority to marketing strategies that yield the best return on investment while taking your budget into account.

You can monitor your progress and make data-driven decisions to maximize your marketing efforts by establishing specific, quantifiable marketing goals.

6.3.2 Clarifying Your Approach to Marketing
It's time to outline the tactics you'll employ to reach your marketing objectives after you've set them. Your target market, brand identity, and available resources should all be reflected in your marketing plans. The following are important marketing tactics to think about:

Material marketing is the process of producing informative, entertaining, or inspirational material for your target audience. Posts on social media, podcasts, videos, infographics, and blogs can all fall under this category. Use a variety of distribution methods to reach and include your target audience with your material.

Social media marketing: Use sites like YouTube, Facebook, Instagram, Twitter, LinkedIn, and Facebook to interact with your audience, increase brand recognition, and increase website traffic. Create a social media content schedule and assess the success of your efforts with analytics.

Optimize your website and content for search engines like Google to raise your organic search ranks. This is known as search engine optimization, or SEO. To improve your visibility and generate organic traffic, carry out keyword research, optimize the content and structure of your website, and create high-quality backlinks.

Email marketing: Create a list of interested clients and prospects, then send them customized and targeted emails. Utilize email marketing tools to track the effectiveness of your communications, categorize your audience, and automate campaigns.

Paid Advertising: To reach a larger audience and increase targeted traffic to your website, think about utilizing paid advertising channels like Google Ads, Facebook Ads, Instagram Ads, and LinkedIn Ads. To get the most out of your advertising expenditure, decide on a budget, identify your target market, and produce eye-catching creatives.

Influencer marketing: Assist influential people in your field who have a sizable and devoted fan base. Join forces with them to market your good or service, and take advantage of their reputation and clout to reach a larger audience.

Public relations (PR): Create connections with bloggers, journalists, and industry influencers to get mentions and attention in the media. To raise the awareness and legitimacy of your brand, write press releases, make story pitching suggestions, and take part in industry gatherings.

Keep in mind that not every marketing tactic will work for your company. Select the tactics that fit your objectives, resources, and target audience. Regularly assess the effectiveness of your marketing initiatives and tweak as necessary to maximize your outcomes.

6.3.3 Establishing a Marketing Budget

Making a budget to allot funds to your marketing initiatives is another aspect of developing a marketing plan. The total budget for your company as well as the anticipated return on investment from your marketing initiatives should be considered when creating your marketing budget.

When drafting a marketing budget, take into account the following:

Marketing Goals: Assign a portion of your total budget according to the significance and precedence of your marketing goals. For instance, you may devote a larger percentage of your money to content marketing and social media advertising if raising brand awareness is your main objective.

Marketing Channels: Take into account the price of any marketing channel you intend to employ. Certain channels, like social media marketing, could be less expensive than more conventional ones, like print or television, for advertising.

Testing and Optimization: Allocate a specific amount of your funds to the testing and improvement of your advertising initiatives. This will enable you to test out various approaches and methods to see which ones are most effective for your company.

Analytics and tracking: To monitor the effectiveness of your marketing initiatives, make an investment in marketing analytics software. In order to maximize your marketing efforts, this will assist you in calculating the return on investment and making data-driven decisions.

Recall to periodically assess and modify your marketing budget in light of your company's evolving needs as well as the effectiveness of your marketing initiatives.

6.3.4 Tracking and Assessing Your Marketing Initiatives
Measuring and assessing the success of your marketing initiatives is essential to the success of your marketing plan. You can determine what is and is not working with your marketing strategy and make well-informed decisions by monitoring important indicators and analyzing the data.

When evaluating your marketing activities, take into account the following important metrics:

Website Traffic: Track the sources of traffic

(organic, direct, referral, social, etc.) and keep an eye on the quantity of people visiting your website. Examine user activity on your website, including page views, bounce rate, and duration of visit.

Conversion Rate: Calculate the proportion of website visitors who complete a desired activity, such as buying something, completing a form, or signing up for your newsletter. Determine which marketing channels and campaigns are most effective by calculating their conversion rates.

Customer Acquisition Cost (CAC): Divide your total marketing spend by the quantity of new clients you have brought on board to get the cost of bringing on a new client. To make sure you're profitable, compare your CAC to the customer's lifetime value.

Return on Investment (ROI): Calculate each marketing campaign's ROI by contrasting the amount of money raised with the campaign's expenses. This will assist you in determining which marketing initiatives and channels are most successful.

Engagement on Social Media: Keep an eye on the data related to likes, comments, shares, and followers on your various social media accounts. Evaluate the results of your social media marketing efforts and modify your plans as necessary.

Email marketing metrics: Monitor your email campaigns' open, click-through, and conversion rates. To maximize the effectiveness of your email marketing campaign, test various call-to-actions, content, and subject lines.

Examine and evaluate these indicators on a regular basis to spot trends, patterns, and potential improvement areas. Make greater use of the knowledge acquired to hone your marketing approaches and techniques.

In summary

One of the most important steps in transforming your idea into a profitable business is creating a marketing plan. You may increase your chances of reaching your target audience, generating leads, and boosting sales by setting clear goals, defining efficient methods, allocating a budget, and tracking your marketing efforts. Recall that marketing is a constant process, so as your company grows, it's critical to continually assess and modify your marketing strategy.

6.4 Making Use of Offline and Internet Marketing Channels

It's time to concentrate on marketing when you have produced your product or service and are prepared to start your firm. Getting clients and making sales depend on effective marketing. Utilizing both online and offline marketing channels is crucial in today's digital world if you want to expand your audience and optimize the potential of your company.

6.4.1 Channels for Online Marketing

The way companies sell their goods and services has been completely transformed by the internet. Numerous options are available through online marketing channels to engage with potential clients and increase brand recognition. Consider the following important internet marketing channels:

1. Internet page

Any firm must have a well-designed and user-friendly website. Your website acts as the public face of your business and gives prospective clients access to information about your offerings. Ensure that your website is search engine optimized, visually appealing, and simple to navigate.

2. SEO, or search engine optimization
The practice of making your website more search engine-friendly is known as SEO. You may increase your website's exposure and draw in organic traffic by using pertinent keywords, producing excellent content, and developing backlinks. To help you optimize your website, think about working with an SEO expert or utilizing online resources.

3. Content Promotion
To draw in and keep your target audience interested, content marketing entails producing and disseminating interesting material. Posts on blogs, articles, videos, infographics, and more can fall under this category. By offering insightful content and proving your expertise in the field, you may win over prospective clients' trust and increase website traffic.

4. Marketing on Social Media
Social media sites with significant marketing potential include Facebook, Instagram, Twitter, and LinkedIn. To engage with your target audience, create business profiles on pertinent platforms and publish interesting material frequently. To advertise your goods and services

and reach a larger audience, use social media.

5. Direct Messaging

Building customer relationships and nurturing leads at a low cost can be achieved through email marketing. To keep your audience informed and interested, gather email addresses via your website or other means, and send out newsletters or promotional emails on a regular basis. To boost open rates and conversions, personalize your emails and offer value.

6. Advertising Pay-Per-Click (PPC)

With pay-per-click (PPC) advertising, you may run advertisements on search engines and other websites and only have to pay when someone clicks on them. With the powerful targeting possibilities provided by platforms like Google Ads and Facebook Ads, you can reach particular demographics and raise your conversion rates. For maximum return on investment, set a budget and track your efforts.

6.4.2 Channels for Offline Marketing

Even though traditional marketing methods are still important for reaching certain consumers, online marketing is still crucial in today's digital environment. Consider the following offline marketing channels:

1. Print Promotion

Print advertising consists of direct mail, brochures, flyers, magazine ads, and newspaper ads. Print advertising can be a useful tool for reaching particular demographics or local clients, depending on who your target audience is. Create visually striking images and persuasive language to draw in customers and spark interest in your company.

2. Functions and Exhibits
Engaging in trade exhibitions and industry events gives you a chance to present your goods or services to a specific audience. Organize a visually appealing booth, interact with guests, and get leads. For more attention and to differentiate yourself from the competition, think about providing unique promos or freebies.

3. Establishing connections
One effective offline marketing tactic is networking, which enables you to establish connections with influential people in the business, partners, and prospective clients. To network with like-minded people and market your firm, go to local business events, seminars, and industry conferences. To leave a lasting impression, bring business cards and an elevator pitch.

4. PR, or public relations
PR entails cultivating a positive image for your company and fostering connections with the media. Create a public relations plan that consists of media outreach, press releases, and attendance at pertinent industry events. Good media

attention can greatly increase the legitimacy of your brand and draw in new clients.

5. Programs for Referrals

Create a program that incentivizes current clients to recommend your company to their friends and acquaintances. To promote referrals, provide rewards like discounts, freebies, or special access. Word-of-mouth advertising has great potential to bring in a constant flow of new clients.

In summary

To reach a larger audience and realize the full potential of your brand, you must combine offline and internet marketing methods. To successfully sell your goods or services, create a thorough marketing plan that combines traditional and digital marketing techniques. Keep a close eye on and evaluate your marketing initiatives to determine what is most effective for your company and make the required changes. Recall that marketing is a continuous process, and the success of your company depends on keeping abreast of the most recent tactics and trends.

BUILDING A STRONG TEAM

7.1 Outlining Duties and Positions

Having a capable and strong team is essential to

the success of any business venture. It is your duty as the company's owner to specify each team member's duties and responsibilities to make sure that everyone is aiming for the same objective. This section will address the significance of clearly defining roles and responsibilities as well as offer suggestions for doing so.

7.1.1 The Significance of Outlining Duties and Positions

It's critical to establish roles and duties within your team for a number of reasons. First of all, it promotes clarity and keeps things simple. Everyone can concentrate on their individual jobs and contribute to the business's overall success when they are aware of what is expected of them. This clarity guarantees that all required tasks are being completed and also helps to avoid redundant efforts.

Defined roles and responsibilities also encourage responsibility. Each team member is more likely to take responsibility for their work and produce outcomes when they are fully aware of their roles. A cohesive and effective team requires a culture of trust and dependability, which is fostered by this responsibility.

Finally, efficient collaboration is made possible by well-defined roles and duties. Team members can collaborate more effectively when they are aware of their own and each other's duties. Better problem-solving, more productivity, and eventually the accomplishment of corporate objectives are the results of this collaboration.

7.1.2 Outlining Duties and Positions
Take into consideration the following actions to properly establish roles and responsibilities within your team:

Step 1: Determine Important Duties and Functions
Determine the essential duties and responsibilities that must be fulfilled by your company first. This could apply to departments like customer service, operations, finance, marketing, and sales. Divide each function into discrete tasks and assign accountability for each task.

Step 2: Align knowledge and experience
Next, make sure that each team member's knowledge and abilities align with the duties at hand. Take into account their skills, background, and advantages. Assign assignments to those who possess the abilities and know-how to complete them successfully. By doing this, you can make sure that every member of the team is operating within their area of competence and maximizing their potential to benefit the company.

Step 3: Identify duties and positions
Clearly state each person's roles and responsibilities after you have determined the tasks and paired them with the relevant team members. This must contain a thorough explanation of their responsibilities, anticipated

results, and any particular dates or objectives they must fulfill. Provide as much detail as you can to eliminate any doubt or misunderstanding.

Step 4: Interact and Record
When it comes to defining roles and responsibilities, communication is essential. Make sure that all team members are aware of their roles and responsibilities by efficiently and clearly conveying them. Team meetings, individual conversations, or written materials like task lists or job descriptions can all be used to accomplish this. As the company develops, it's crucial to periodically assess and revise these roles and duties.

7.1.3 Giving and Getting Direction
Clearly defining roles and duties helps your team members accept responsibility for their work in addition to task delegation. A key component of effective leadership is delegation. In addition to reducing your own workload, assigning duties and responsibilities to your team members allows them to advance their careers.

Giving your team members the opportunity to take initiative and make decisions while still setting clear expectations and guidelines is crucial when delegating. Have faith in their skills and, when required, offer assistance and direction. Not only will this empowerment boost their job satisfaction, but it will also instill a sense of ownership and dedication to the company's success.

7.1.4 Cooperation with Teams with Different Functions

It's critical to promote cooperation and cross-functional teamwork, in addition to clearly outlining roles and duties within particular functions. Expertise and input from several business areas are needed for numerous activities and initiatives. By encouraging teamwork, you may make the most of the many backgrounds and viewpoints of your members to stimulate creativity and solve problems.

Provide your team members from various departments with the chance to collaborate on projects or initiatives. Promote respectful interaction, knowledge exchange, and open communication. In addition to improving the caliber of the job, this cross-functional cooperation will fortify the relationships within your team.

In summary

One of the most important steps in creating a solid and competent team is defining roles and responsibilities. You may establish a productive and cooperative work atmosphere by giving your team members clear instructions, matching abilities and expertise, and providing them with authority. As your company grows, don't forget to periodically evaluate and update roles and responsibilities. You should also promote cross-functional cooperation to spur creativity and success.

7.2 Recruiting and Hiring the Right People

Building a strong team is crucial for the success of your business. As an entrepreneur, you can't do everything on your own, and hiring the right people is essential to help you achieve your goals. In this section, we will discuss the process of recruiting and hiring the right individuals for your team.

7.2.1 Defining the Roles and Responsibilities

Before you start recruiting, it's important to clearly define the roles and responsibilities within your organization. This will help you identify the specific skills and qualifications you are looking for in potential candidates. Take the time to create detailed job descriptions that outline the key responsibilities and requirements for each position.

When defining the roles, consider the current and future needs of your business. Think about the tasks that need to be accomplished and the skills that are necessary to fulfill those tasks. This will ensure that you hire individuals who are the right fit for your organization and can contribute to its growth.

7.2.2 Creating a Recruitment Strategy

Once you have a clear understanding of the roles

you need to fill, it's time to develop a recruitment strategy. This involves determining where and how you will find potential candidates. There are several methods you can use to attract talent, including:

1. Job boards and online platforms: Post your job openings on popular job boards and online platforms such as LinkedIn, Indeed, and Glassdoor. These platforms allow you to reach a wide audience and attract candidates who are actively looking for job opportunities.

2. Networking: Leverage your professional network to find potential candidates. Attend industry events, join relevant groups and associations, and connect with individuals who have the skills and experience you are looking for. Referrals from trusted contacts can often lead to high-quality candidates.

3. Social media: Utilize social media platforms like Facebook, Twitter, and Instagram to promote your job openings. Share engaging content about your company culture and values to attract candidates who align with your organization's mission.

4. Recruitment agencies: Consider partnering with recruitment agencies that specialize in your industry. These agencies have

access to a wide network of candidates and can help you find individuals who meet your specific requirements.

5. University and college career centers: Reach out to career centers at local universities and colleges to connect with recent graduates who may be looking for job opportunities. This can be a great way to find young talent with fresh perspectives and a willingness to learn.

7.2.3 Screening and Interviewing Candidates

Once you start receiving applications, it's time to screen and interview potential candidates. This process is crucial in determining whether an individual is the right fit for your organization. Here are some steps you can follow:

1. Review resumes and cover letters: Carefully review each applicant's resume and cover letter to assess their qualifications and experience. Look for relevant skills, education, and previous work experience that align with the requirements of the role.

2. Conduct phone or video interviews: Before inviting candidates for in-person interviews, consider conducting phone or video interviews to further assess their suitability. This can help you narrow down your list of potential candidates and save time.

3. In-person interviews: Invite the most promising candidates for in-person interviews. Prepare a list of questions that will help you evaluate their skills, experience, and cultural fit. Consider conducting multiple rounds of interviews to get a comprehensive understanding of each candidate.

4. Assess cultural fit: In addition to evaluating skills and qualifications, it's important to assess whether a candidate will fit well within your company culture. Ask questions that will help you gauge their values, work ethic, and ability to collaborate with others.

7.2.4 Making the Hiring Decision

After completing the screening and interviewing process, it's time to make the hiring decision. Consider the following factors when making your final decision:

1. Skills and qualifications: Evaluate each candidate's skills and qualifications in relation to the requirements of the role. Choose individuals who have the necessary expertise to contribute to the success of your business.

2. Cultural fit: Assess whether the candidate aligns with your company culture and values. A strong cultural fit can lead to

better teamwork and increased employee satisfaction.

3. Potential for growth: Look for candidates who have the potential to grow and develop within your organization. Hiring individuals who are eager to learn and take on new challenges can contribute to the long-term success of your business.

4. References and background checks: Before extending an offer, conduct reference checks and background checks to verify the information provided by the candidate. This can help you ensure that you are making a well-informed decision.

7.2.5 Onboarding and Training

Once you have hired the right individuals, it's important to provide them with a smooth onboarding and training process. This will help them integrate into your team and understand their roles and responsibilities. Consider the following steps:

1. Provide an orientation: Introduce new hires to your company's mission, values, and culture. Give them an overview of the organization's structure and introduce them to their team members.

2. Assign a mentor: Pair new hires with a mentor who can guide them through their

initial days and weeks. This will help them feel supported and provide them with someone they can turn to for guidance.

3. Training and development: Provide ongoing training and development opportunities to help your employees enhance their skills and stay up-to-date with industry trends. This can include workshops, seminars, online courses, and mentoring programs.

4. Regular feedback and performance evaluations: Establish a system for providing regular feedback and conducting performance evaluations. This will help you identify areas for improvement and provide your employees with the guidance they need to succeed.

By following these steps, you can recruit and hire the right people for your team. Remember, building a strong team is essential for the success of your business, so take the time to find individuals who are the right fit for your organization's goals and values.

7.3 Fostering a Positive Work Environment

Creating a positive workplace culture is crucial to your business's long-term growth and profitability. A company with a great culture not only draws and keeps top people, but it also cultivates a motivated and productive workforce. This section will discuss the value of developing a positive workplace culture and offer doable tactics for establishing an atmosphere that fosters creativity, teamwork, and employee happiness.

7.3.1 Establishing Your Organizational Values

Establishing your company's values is the first step towards creating a positive culture. The guiding ideals that direct behavior and decision-making inside your company are known as company values. These principles ought to be consistent with your goals and mission, as well as the culture you hope to foster.

Consider your priorities as a leader and business owner before defining your company's principles.

Think about the core ideas and tenets that guide your company. Your staff should be able to relate to and live up to these principles. Once your company's values have been determined, make sure your workforce is aware of them and incorporates them into day-to-day operations.

7.3.2 Setting an Example

You, as a leader or business owner, are vital to forming the culture of your organization. The tone that is set for the entire organization is determined by your actions and conduct. Setting an example for others to follow entails modeling the attitudes and conduct you desire from your staff.

Show honesty, openness, and decency in all of your dealings. Promote candid dialogue and teamwork among members of the team. Employees that exhibit the desired behaviors and values should be acknowledged and rewarded. You may encourage and inspire your team to adopt the same culture by continuously exhibiting it yourself.

7.3.3 Creating a Feeling of Acceptance

Developing a positive organizational culture requires fostering a sense of belonging. Employee engagement and commitment to their work are more likely when they feel appreciated, a part of the company, and linked.

Establish chances for teamwork and collaboration to promote a feeling of inclusion. Encourage staff members to voice their thoughts and opinions and pay attention to what they have to say. Honor variety and establish a welcoming atmosphere where everyone is treated with dignity and gratitude. You can build a cohesive and encouraging team that collaborates to achieve a common objective by fostering a sense of belonging.

7.3.4 Encouraging Equilibrium Work-Life

Encouraging work-life balance is essential for the happiness and well-being of employees. Employees can refuel, lower their stress levels, and preserve their general wellbeing when they have a healthy work-life balance. Workers are more likely to be engaged and productive when they feel encouraged to achieve work-life balance.

Encourage staff members to emphasize self-care, take breaks, and maximize their vacation time. Whenever feasible, provide flexible work options like remote work or adjustable hours. Set boundaries and show your staff that you value work-life balance by showing that you respect their personal time. Fostering a work-life balance will help you establish an environment where your staff members' general wellbeing is valued.

7.3.5 Promoting Ongoing Education and Growth

Establishing a culture of ongoing education and training is crucial to the development and satisfaction of staff members. Employees feel appreciated and inspired to contribute to the success of the company when they get the chance to learn and acquire new skills.

Provide training and development opportunities that complement your company's demands and the career aspirations of your staff. Encourage staff members to take advantage of chances for professional development and assist them in their development. Encourage a culture of learning by offering mentorship opportunities, encouraging knowledge exchange, and praising and rewarding staff members who make personal development efforts. You can foster an innovative and expanding culture by supporting ongoing learning and development.

7.3.6 Honoring Successes and Milestones

Celebrating successes and turning points is a big component of creating a healthy work environment. Acknowledging and honoring staff members' achievements improves morale and supports the ideals and behaviors that the company wants to see in its members.

Celebrate successes both as a team and as individuals to foster a culture of celebration. Establish a program of appreciation that honors exceptional achievements and accomplishments. Celebrate big victories, such as finishing a project, celebrating an anniversary, or accomplishing crucial business objectives. You may cultivate an environment of gratitude and inspiration by acknowledging and commemorating accomplishments.

7.3.7 Promoting Input and Ongoing Enhancement

Promoting feedback and ongoing development is essential to creating a positive workplace culture. Employees become active contributors to the success of the company when they are given the confidence to voice their opinions and offer feedback.

Establish avenues for direct and honest communication, such as anonymous surveys, suggestion boxes, and frequent team meetings. Pay attention to the opinions and suggestions made by your staff members. Encourage a culture of continuous improvement by putting feedback loops in place and routinely evaluating and improving procedures and methods. You can cultivate a culture of creativity and adaptability by promoting feedback and ongoing improvement.

7.3.8 Promoting Workers' Well-Being

Providing for the well-being of employees is essential to creating a pleasant workplace culture. Employee engagement and productivity are higher when they feel that their physical, mental, and emotional well-being is encouraged.

Provide access to mental health resources, mindfulness workshops, fitness challenges, and other wellness initiatives that support a healthy lifestyle. Establish a welcoming and secure work environment where the health and safety of employees come first. Recognize and respect the personal struggles that your employees are facing, and offer assistance when required. You may cultivate an environment where workers are valued and cared for by promoting their well-being.

7.3.9 Keeping an Upbeat and Helpful Environment
Keeping the atmosphere upbeat and encouraging is crucial to creating a positive workplace culture. Establish an environment where workers feel free to share their thoughts, seek assistance, and take chances.

Encourage cooperation and teamwork by cultivating a climate of respect and trust. Promote honest and helpful communication, and deal with disagreements or problems quickly and equitably. Offer prospects for career progression and growth, and assist staff members in realizing their career goals. Employee engagement and loyalty can be fostered by cultivating a culture that is positive and helpful.

Although creating a great workplace culture requires time and work, the benefits are priceless. In addition to drawing and keeping top people, a positive workplace culture promotes creativity, productivity, and general corporate success. You will have no trouble establishing a work atmosphere that motivates and encourages your staff to perform to the best of their abilities if you adhere to the tactics discussed in this section.

7.4 Encouraging and Maintaining Staff Members
Creating a solid team is crucial to any company's success. But keeping your staff motivated and engaged is just as crucial. Your team members are more likely to be creative, productive, and dedicated to the success of your company when they are inspired and involved. This section will discuss methods for inspiring and holding onto workers in order to establish a productive and happy workplace.

7.4.1 Acknowledge and Honor Successes
Acknowledging and rewarding employees for their accomplishments is one of the best strategies to keep them motivated. Employees are more likely to be driven to give their best work when they feel respected and appreciated. Congratulating someone on a job well done and extending praise are easy ways to acknowledge accomplishments. In addition, think about putting in place a rewards system that recognizes great work or accomplished goals. This could involve rewards like bonuses, promotions, or other incentives that fit the ambitions and goals of your staff members.

7.4.2 Offer chances for advancement and progress. When given the chance to grow and develop, employees are more likely to remain motivated and engaged. Provide workshops, seminars, and training courses to improve their expertise. Encourage staff members to establish their own objectives, both personal and professional, and make sure they have the tools and assistance they need to succeed. Furthermore, think about setting up a mentorship program where senior staff members can assist and mentor junior team members. By supporting your staff members' personal and professional development, you not only inspire them but also forge a more cohesive and competent team.

7.4.3 Encourage a Happy and Healthy Workplace

Employee motivation and retention are greatly impacted by a favorable work environment. Establish a culture that values cooperation, candor, and respect. Promote cooperation among staff members and provide them chances to mingle and get to know their coworkers. Encourage a sense of community and ensure that each member of the team feels appreciated and involved. Additionally, encourage a positive and healthy work environment and pay attention to work-life balance. Employees are more likely to be motivated and dedicated to the company's success when they feel supported and pleased at work.

7.4.4 Assign and Empower

Giving workers more authority and assigning them tasks can be effective ways to inspire them. Employees are more likely to be motivated and engaged when they feel trusted, empowered, and given responsibility for their work. Give them the authority and tools they need to succeed by assigning them jobs and projects that fit their interests and skill sets. Promote employee autonomy and provide them with the freedom to experiment and come up with fresh ideas. Giving your team members more authority not only inspires them but also promotes a proactive and innovative culture.

7.4.5 Promote a Balanced Work-Life

Sustaining a positive work-life equilibrium is crucial for the motivation and overall well-being of employees. Encourage staff members to emphasize self-care, take breaks, and maximize their vacation time. Don't put too much pressure on staff members or set unreasonable expectations. Schedules should be flexible, and if remote work is an option, it should be considered. You may demonstrate to your staff that you appreciate their well-being and understand the significance of their personal lives by encouraging work-life balance. Increased motivation and loyalty follow from this.

7.4.6 Communicate frequently and seek input.

A critical component of employee motivation and retention is effective communication. Maintain open lines of communication with your team members to answer any queries or issues they may have, as well as to share information and updates. Establish a comfortable environment where staff members can freely share their thoughts and opinions. Encourage candid and frank feedback. As you actively hear what they have to say, respond appropriately. Incorporating employees into decision-making procedures and esteeming their opinions not only inspires them but also cultivates a feeling of loyalty and ownership towards the company.

7.4.7 Encourage the Integration of Work and Life

The ability to integrate work and life is becoming more and more crucial in the fast-paced world of today. Encourage staff members to develop methods to combine their personal and professional lives rather than seeing them as two distinct things. Provide employees with flexible work schedules that let them take care of personal problems in addition to their job obligations. Encourage a culture that helps employees strike a healthy balance between work and life and places a high value on it. Encouragement of work-life integration fosters an atmosphere that values and upholds workers' personal lives, which boosts motivation and contentment.

7.4.8 Periodically Assess and Modify

Employee motivation and retention are continuous processes. Assess the success of your tactics on a regular basis and adapt as necessary. Ask for input from staff members to find out what inspires them and what needs work. Keep abreast of market developments and the latest techniques for retaining and inspiring employees. You can make sure that your staff members stay involved and motivated by regularly reviewing and tweaking your strategy, which will increase productivity and help your firm succeed.

In summary, keeping and inspiring staff members is essential to your company's success. You can build a motivated and engaged team that is dedicated to the success of your company by rewarding achievement, offering chances for learning and improvement, creating a positive work environment, giving authority and delegating, encouraging work-life balance, communicating and getting feedback on a regular basis, promoting work-life integration, and routinely evaluating and making adjustments. Recall that fulfilling and inspired workers are essential to making your ideal career a reality.

ADAPTING AND ITERATING YOUR BUSINESS STRATEGY

8.1 Tracking Shifts and Trends in the Market

It is critical for entrepreneurs to keep up with developments and trends in the market, given how quickly the business landscape is changing. You may stay ahead of the competition, make wise judgments, and modify your company plan by keeping an eye on these changes. This part will address the significance of keeping an eye on market developments and trends, as well as practical methods for doing so.

8.1.1 The Importance of Market Surveillance

Changes and trends in the market can have a big effect on your company. You may spot new opportunities, predict client wants, and proactively change your goods, services, and marketing tactics by keeping abreast of these changes. For the following reasons, keeping an eye on market developments is essential:

Finding new chances: You might find new chances that fit with your business objectives by closely monitoring market developments. For example, you might look for ways to include eco-friendly techniques in your offers if you see a growing demand for sustainable items.

Recognizing Customer Needs: Shifts in customer preferences and behavior are frequently reflected in market movements. You can predict customer wants and adjust your products or services by keeping an eye on these patterns. By taking a proactive stance, you may maintain your competitive edge and cultivate a devoted clientele.

Remaining Competitive: It's critical to maintain your competitiveness in a business climate that is changing quickly. You can learn how your competitors are doing and come up with unique ideas by keeping an eye on market trends. With this insight, you can stay ahead of the competition and provide distinctive value offers.

Adapting to Technological Developments: New possibilities and industry disruptions might result from technological breakthroughs. You can keep up with evolving technology and choose how to incorporate it into your organization by keeping an eye on industry trends. This flexibility guarantees that your operations are future-proof and that you stay relevant.

8.1.2 Techniques for Tracking Changes and Trends in the Market

Now that we know how crucial it is to keep an eye on market trends, let's examine some practical methods for being informed and making data-driven choices:

Industry Research: Learn everything there is to know about your industry's present situation and expected future growth. Keep up with industry journals, reports, and news to learn about consumer behavior, market trends, and emerging technology. You'll be able to see opportunities and make wise judgments with the aid of this research.

Analyze your competitors' strategy, product lines, and clientele by keeping a careful watch on them. Examine their advantages and disadvantages to find places where you can set yourself apart. You can remain ahead of industry trends and strategically modify your business by keeping an eye on your competition.

Customer input: In order to understand your consumers' wants, preferences, and pain spots, actively seek out their input. Engage with your customers on a regular basis to gain insightful information through focus groups, surveys, and social media. You may use this feedback to spot new trends and develop your goods and services in a way that puts the needs of your customers first.

Attend trade exhibitions, industry conferences, and networking events to meet business leaders and learn about the newest developments in the field. To get insightful information, have talks, take part in panel discussions, and pay attention to keynote speakers. Making connections with pros in the field might provide you with new insights and keep you on the cutting edge.

Data analytics: Monitor and evaluate important performance indicators (KPIs) for your company by using data analytics technologies. To spot patterns and trends, track data like sales, website traffic, customer involvement, and social media interactions. You can optimize your business plans and make well-informed decisions with the help of data-driven insights.

Social listening: Keep an eye on online forums, social media platforms, and website reviews to gauge user opinion and spot new trends. You may monitor mentions of your brand, industry terms, and rival activity with the aid of social listening technologies. Engaging in active listening during online chats can help you obtain important insights and efficiently address consumer needs.

Industry Thought Leaders: Check out the blogs, podcasts, and social media accounts of thought leaders, experts, and influencers in the field. These people frequently offer insightful commentary, forecasts, and trend analysis. Maintaining a network with thought leaders can help you stay up-to-date on the most recent advancements in your field and acquire new insights.

8.1.3 Making Use of Market Intelligence

It is only beneficial to track industry trends and developments if you use the knowledge you obtain to motivate significant action. Here are a few strategies for making efficient use of market insights:

Product and Service Development: When creating new goods or services, take market research into consideration. Find market gaps and fill them with products and services that suit the demands and tastes of your target audience. Fitting your products and services with current market trends improves your chances of success and client happiness.

Marketing and Communication: Make sure your strategy for marketing and communication takes market findings into account. Create messages that are specifically tailored to your audience, speaking to their problems. You may successfully reach and interact with consumers by coordinating your marketing initiatives with current market trends.

Business Strategy: Modify your plan in light of market developments. Determine what has to be improved, investigate untapped markets, and modify your distribution or price plans accordingly. You may set up your business for development and success by matching your business plan with current market trends.

Collaborations and Partnerships: Using market knowledge, identify possible joint ventures or partnerships. Seek out related companies or industry participants who can assist you in broadening your customer base or improving your products. You can create mutually beneficial strategic collaborations by utilizing market insights.

In conclusion, keeping an eye on market

developments and trends is critical to your company's success. You can spot new opportunities, anticipate client demands, and modify your methods as necessary if you keep yourself updated. Use the tactics covered in this section to keep an eye on market trends, and use the knowledge you gather to motivate actionable steps. Continue to be proactive, welcome change, and set up your company for long-term success.

8.2 Assessing and Examining Your Company's Performance

After your company has been operating, it's critical to periodically assess and scrutinize its performance. This will enable you to recognize your venture's strong and weak points, make wise decisions, and guarantee its long-term success. We'll go over the main techniques and procedures for assessing and analyzing your company's performance in this part.

8.2.1 Choosing KPIs (Key Performance Indicators)

Setting up key performance indicators (KPIs) is crucial for conducting an efficient assessment of your company's performance. KPIs are quantifiable objectives that represent the essential elements of your company's success. They offer a precise framework for evaluating your development and pinpointing areas in need of improvement.

It's critical to take into account both non-financial and financial variables while establishing KPIs. Financial KPIs give you information about your company's financial health. Examples include revenue growth, profit margin, and return on investment. Non-financial KPIs provide a more comprehensive view of your total performance, including staff engagement, customer satisfaction, and brand recognition.

Take into consideration your industry, business strategy, and strategic objectives to identify the KPIs that are most pertinent to your company. For instance, you would want to monitor metrics like conversion rate, average order value, and customer lifetime value if you are managing an online store. If you work in the service sector, however, you could be more interested in indicators like client referrals, service quality, and retention rates.

8.2.2 Gathering and Examining Information
The next step after determining your KPIs is to gather and examine the relevant data. This entails

compiling data from a range of sources, including staff input, financial documents, customer surveys, and website analytics. Ensuring the precision and dependability of your data is crucial for making well-informed decisions.

Effective data collection and analysis can be facilitated by a variety of technologies and applications. You can use accounting software or engage a professional accountant to obtain financial data. You can use online survey platforms or customer relationship management (CRM) systems to obtain customer data. Furthermore, online analytics programs such as Google Analytics can offer insightful data on user behavior, website traffic, and conversion rates.

It's time to examine the data after you've gathered it in order to get valuable insights. To better understand your business performance, look for correlations, patterns, and trends. For instance, you can look into potential causes and take corrective action if you observe a drop in customer satisfaction ratings. In a similar vein, if you notice an increase in website traffic but a low conversion rate, you may want to look into ways to enhance the user experience and sales funnel optimization.

8.2.3 Performance Comparing and Benchmarking
Benchmarking is an important technique for assessing how well your company is performing in comparison to competitors or industry norms. You can determine your strengths and weaknesses

by evaluating your performance against industry standards. This will enable you to prioritize your efforts for progress, set reasonable targets, and keep one step ahead of the competition.

Finding the important performance indicators that are pertinent to your sector is the first step in benchmarking your performance. Industry groups, online databases, and market research papers are good places to find industry benchmarks. Examine the differences between your performance and these benchmarks. This will enable you to see exactly where you are and where you need to grow.

Internal benchmarking can also be carried out by contrasting your present performance with previous results. This enables you to monitor your development over time and spot patterns or trends. For instance, if your revenue has been rising steadily over the past few years, your business methods are working. However, if your profit margin has been dropping, you might need to make changes to your pricing or implement cost-cutting strategies.

8.2.4 Performing a SWOT evaluation

A SWOT analysis is an effective method for analyzing the opportunities, threats, weaknesses, and strengths of your company. It gives you a thorough picture of both your internal and external market situations, empowering you to create strategies and make well-informed decisions.

The first step in performing a SWOT analysis is to determine the advantages and disadvantages of your company. These are internal variables, like your USP, staff of talent, or effective procedures, that you can manage. Next, determine the challenges and possibilities present in your external environment, including any new competitors, developing industry trends, or evolving legal requirements.

Examine these aspects' effects on the performance of your firm after you've recognized them. A strong internet presence and a devoted clientele, for instance, are signs of a competitive edge. However, your market share might be threatened if your business is extremely crowded and there is fierce rivalry.

You may improve your awareness of your company's place in the market and create plans to take advantage of opportunities, reduce threats, strengthen your position, and capitalize on your weaknesses by performing a SWOT analysis.

8.2.5 Requesting Input and Ongoing Enhancement

It is imperative to obtain input from your customers, staff, and other stakeholders in addition to conducting data analysis and strategy evaluation. Their viewpoints and thoughts might offer insightful information on the state of your company and potential areas for development.

Through focus groups, online reviews, and questionnaires, you can get input from your customers. You may use this feedback to better understand consumer satisfaction levels, pinpoint problems, and find areas where your product or service could be improved. In a similar vein, staff input can reveal details about the efficiency of your internal procedures, team dynamics, and corporate culture in general.

Pay attention to what others have to say and consider it when making decisions. Make use of it as a foundation for ongoing innovation and development. Your business plan can be improved by including feedback to make sure you are fulfilling the requirements and expectations of both clients and staff.

In summary

Analyzing and assessing the success of your company is a continuous process that calls for constant observation, data analysis, and strategic assessment. You can learn a great deal about the advantages, disadvantages, opportunities, and dangers facing your company by defining KPIs, gathering and evaluating data, benchmarking your performance, performing SWOT analysis, and getting input from others. This will help you make wise choices, spot opportunities for development, and ensure the long-term viability of your business. Recall that maintaining competitiveness in the fast-paced business environment of today requires ongoing assessment and change.

8.3 Finding Opportunities for Development

Once your company is operating, it's critical to regularly assess its performance and pinpoint areas for development. By using this technique, you can maintain your competitive edge, adjust to shifting market trends, and guarantee the long-term viability of your company. This section will discuss some methods for determining what needs to be changed and how to make those changes.

8.3.1 Examining Customer Input Your customers are among the best sources of information when it comes to pinpointing areas that need work. Engaging in proactive consumer feedback collection and analysis can yield insightful information about your company's strengths and areas for development. Customers' opinions can be gathered in a few different ways:

Surveys: Make surveys and send them out to your clients in order to get their feedback. Surveys should be brief and targeted in order to promote participation.

Testimonials and reviews: Keep an eye on social media and internet review sites to get input from clients who have already dealt with your company. Take note of both favorable and unfavorable feedback to pinpoint areas in need of development.

Interactions with customer service: Whether communicating with customer service via phone, email, or live chat, pay special attention to what goes on. Keep an eye out for complaints or persistent problems that can point to areas that need work.

Following the collection of client feedback, examine the information to find any trends or recurring themes. Seek out places where clients routinely voice their displeasure or offer suggestions for change. Make a list of the most important areas for improvement, and use this information to prioritize them.

8.3.2 Tracking KPIs, or key performance indicators
Measurable measurements that show how well your company is performing are called key performance indicators, or KPIs. You may pinpoint the areas of your company where it is succeeding and those that require improvement by routinely

reviewing KPIs. Typical KPIs to think about are as follows:

Sales revenue: Keep an eye on your sales income to gauge the general financial well-being of your company. To find areas where sales might be dropping or have potential for development, identify trends and patterns.

Determine the cost of obtaining each new customer by using the customer acquisition cost (CAC) method. A high CAC could be a sign that your sales or marketing procedures aren't working well enough.

Calculate your customer retention rate by dividing the total number of clients you have over a given time period. Low retention rates might be a sign of poor customer service or problems with client satisfaction.

Conversion rate: Monitor the proportion of leads or website visitors who become actual, paying customers. A low conversion rate could be a symptom of problems with the messaging, sales process, or design of your website.

By keeping a regular eye on these KPIs, you may spot areas in which your company is underperforming and implement remedial measures to boost output.

8.3.3 Performing Internal Examinations
To find areas for improvement, internal audits

entail a methodical examination of your company's operations, systems, and business processes. You can find inefficiencies, bottlenecks, and places where resources aren't being used to their full potential with this approach. The steps to carry out an internal audit are as follows:

Establish the scope by deciding which particular areas or procedures you wish to audit. This could apply to departments like marketing, operations, finance, and customer service.

Collect information: Gather pertinent information and supporting documentation about the procedures or locations you are auditing. Financial statements, operational reports, and employee or customer feedback are a few examples of this.

Examine the information: Examine the data to find any inconsistencies, inefficiencies, or places that need improvement. Seek chances to improve production, cut expenses, or streamline procedures.

Create an action plan. Create an action plan outlining the required adjustments or enhancements based on your findings. Sort the actions into priority lists according to their viability and possible impact.

Put into practice and keep an eye on: Make the required adjustments and keep an eye on their success. To guarantee continual improvement, examine and update your internal audit procedure on a regular basis.

8.3.4 Requesting Employee Input

Being at the forefront of your company, your staff frequently has insightful knowledge on areas that could use development. Promote open communication and set up avenues for staff members to offer comments and ideas. Regular team meetings, anonymous suggestion boxes, or one-on-one conversations can all help achieve this.

You can pinpoint areas where procedures can be streamlined, communication can be strengthened, or training can be given by proactively seeking out and taking into account employee feedback. Employees that feel empowered and engaged are more inclined to support your company's growth and point out areas for development.

8.3.5 Comparing Your Work to That of Others

Comparing your company's performance to that of your rivals or industry norms is known as benchmarking. You can determine areas where your company may be lagging behind or where you have a competitive advantage by comparing it to others.

Do some competition research to learn about their offerings, costs, marketing plans, and client testimonials. Examine this data against your own company to find out where you stand out or can make improvements. You can use this study to find market gaps, potential areas for innovation, or joint venture prospects.

Recall that the purpose of pinpointing areas for development is to consistently improve and expand your company, not to point fingers or point out flaws. Accept criticism from both clients and staff, and be willing to make the required adjustments. You can maintain an advantage over the competition and bring your firm to long-term success by regularly reviewing and making improvements.

8.4 Implementing Changes and Innovations

Once your business is up and running, it's important to remember that the journey doesn't end there. In order to stay competitive and continue growing, you must be willing to adapt and innovate. Implementing changes and innovations is a crucial step in ensuring the long-term success of your business. This section will guide you through the process of implementing changes and innovations effectively.

8.4.1 Embracing a Culture of Innovation

In order to implement changes and innovations successfully, it's important to foster a culture of innovation within your organization. This starts with creating an environment where new ideas are encouraged and valued. Encourage your employees to think outside the box and come up with creative solutions to problems. Foster a culture of collaboration and open communication, where everyone feels comfortable sharing their ideas and opinions.

8.4.2 Identifying Areas for Improvement

Before implementing any changes or innovations, it's important to identify the areas of your business that need improvement. This can be done through regular evaluation and analysis of your business performance. Look for any bottlenecks, inefficiencies, or areas where you are falling short of your goals. By identifying these areas, you can prioritize your efforts and focus on making the necessary changes.

8.4.3 Setting Clear Objectives

Once you have identified the areas for improvement, it's important to set clear objectives for the changes and innovations you want to implement. These objectives should be specific, measurable, achievable, relevant, and time-bound (SMART). By setting clear objectives, you can track your progress and ensure that you are moving in the right direction.

8.4.4 Developing an Implementation Plan

Implementing changes and innovations requires careful planning and execution. Develop a detailed implementation plan that outlines the steps you need to take, the resources required, and the timeline for implementation. Assign responsibilities to team members and ensure that everyone is clear on their roles and tasks. Regularly review and update your implementation plan as needed.

8.4.5 Communicating the Changes

Effective communication is key when implementing changes and innovations. Clearly communicate the reasons behind the changes and the benefits they will bring to the organization. Be transparent and open with your employees, customers, and stakeholders about the changes you are making. Address any concerns or questions they may have and provide regular updates on the progress of the implementation.

8.4.6 Testing and Iterating

Before fully implementing changes and innovations, it's important to test them on a smaller scale. This allows you to identify any potential issues or challenges and make necessary adjustments. Gather feedback from your employees and customers and use it to refine your changes. Iterate and improve upon your initial ideas until you are confident that they will bring the desired results.

8.4.7 Training and Support

Implementing changes and innovations often requires your employees to learn new skills or adapt to new processes. Provide the necessary training and support to ensure a smooth transition. Offer workshops, seminars, or online courses to help your employees develop the skills they need. Provide ongoing support and guidance as they navigate the changes.

8.4.8 Monitoring and Evaluation

Once the changes and innovations have been implemented, it's important to monitor their effectiveness and evaluate their impact on your business. Set up key performance indicators (KPIs) to track the progress and measure the success of the changes. Regularly review and analyze the data to identify any areas that need further improvement or adjustment.

8.4.9 Celebrating Success and Learning from Failure

When implementing changes and innovations, it's important to celebrate the successes along the way. Recognize and reward the efforts of your team members who have contributed to the success of the changes. At the same time, it's important to learn from any failures or setbacks. Use them as opportunities for growth and improvement, and adjust your approach accordingly.

8.4.10 Embracing Continuous Improvement

Implementing changes and innovations is not a one-time event. It's an ongoing process that requires continuous improvement. Encourage a mindset of continuous learning and improvement within your organization. Regularly review and evaluate your business processes and look for ways to make them more efficient and effective. Stay up to date with industry trends and changes, and be willing to adapt and innovate as needed.

By implementing changes and innovations effectively, you can ensure the long-term success and growth of your business. Embrace a culture of innovation, identify areas for improvement, set clear objectives, develop an implementation plan, communicate the changes, test and iterate, provide training and support, monitor and evaluate, celebrate success, learn from failure, and embrace continuous improvement. With these strategies in place, you will be well-equipped to navigate the ever-changing business landscape and stay ahead of the competition.

Scaling Your Business

9.1 Comprehending the Process of Growth

After launching your business and building a strong foundation, it's time to concentrate on growing your operations and reaching new markets. Growing your company is an exciting journey that needs to be carefully planned and carried out. We'll look at the growth process in this section and give you some tips on how to scale your firm successfully.

9.1.1 Determining Growth Objectives

Setting goals for your improvement is crucial

before you start the trip. These objectives will direct and function as a road map for your decision-making. Establish your target revenue, market share, and customer acquisition objectives first. You may monitor your progress and make well-informed decisions to attain sustainable growth by establishing specific, quantifiable goals.

9.1.2 Reaching a Wider Audience

One of the most important parts of growing your business is reaching new markets. It entails breaking into undiscovered markets and attracting new clients. Take into account these tactics in order to increase your market reach:

Market segmentation: Examine your intended market to find new niches for your good or service. Adapt your marketing strategies to these segments' particular demands and preferences.

Geographic Expansion: If your company just works in one area, think about going to other places. Create a localized marketing plan by conducting market research to determine which places have a high demand for your products or services.

Partnerships and Alliances: To increase your reach, work with firms that complement yours or establish strategic alliances. You can reach a larger audience and access their current consumer base by collaborating with well-known businesses or influencers.

Online Presence: Use digital channels to reach a wider audience. Using content marketing, SEO, and social media marketing, establish a powerful online presence. To draw in new clients, interact with your target audience by providing insightful and pertinent material.

9.1.3 Handling a Rise in Demand

There will be a rise in demand for your goods or services as your company grows. In order to guarantee client happiness and uphold a favorable reputation, it is imperative to handle this rising demand in an efficient manner. Think about the following tactics:

Streamline Operations: Examine your current procedures and pinpoint opportunities for improvement. Optimize your processes to enhance productivity and satisfy the growing demand without sacrificing quality.

Supply network management: To guarantee a constant flow of inventory, fortify your supply network. To prevent stockouts and delays, build dependable supplier relationships and put inventory management mechanisms in place.

Customer service: Make an investment in customer service to give your expanding clientele outstanding support. Teach the members of your customer service staff to rapidly address and resolve client inquiries. Put in place systems for collecting consumer feedback so you can keep improving your products and services.

Scalable Infrastructure: Evaluate your infrastructure requirements and upgrade as needed to meet growing demand. This could entail buying more equipment, improving your technological systems, or increasing your physical space.

9.1.4 Infrastructure and Operational Scaling

It takes meticulous planning and operational strategy execution to scale your firm. To efficiently scale your operations and infrastructure, take into account the following strategies:

Automation: To optimize your operations, identify repetitive jobs and investigate automation solutions. Process automation can lower expenses, increase productivity, and free up resources for other crucial areas of your company.

Assess which of your company's non-core operations can be contracted out to outside service providers. You may scale more effectively and concentrate on your main business by outsourcing support functions like accounting, IT, and customer service.

Technology Integration: Adopt technological solutions to boost productivity and improve operations. Streamlining procedures and promoting expansion can be achieved through the use of project management tools, CRM software, and enterprise resource planning (ERP) systems.

Training and Development: Make an investment in programs that will upskill your staff and provide them with the know-how to support the expansion of your company. Your team will be able to contribute to the scaling process and adjust to shifting demands with the support of ongoing professional development and learning.

Growing your company is a thrilling and difficult task. You can successfully navigate this phase by comprehending the growth process and putting good strategies into practice. Don't forget to handle rising demand, broaden your market reach, scale your operations and infrastructure, and create clear growth targets. You can land your dream job and position your company for long-term success with careful planning and execution.

9.2: Broadening Your Consumer Base

A vital first step in growing your company and attaining long-term success is reaching a wider audience. To expand your consumer base and boost income as your company expands, it's critical to investigate new markets and connect with a larger audience. This section will cover a variety of techniques and approaches that can effectively broaden your market reach.

9.2.1 Find Fresh Target Audiences

Finding new target audiences that complement

your offerings of goods or services is necessary if you want to increase your market reach. To learn about the needs, tastes, and habits of potential clients in these new marketplaces, conduct market research. This will assist you in modifying your marketing tactics and messaging so that they speak to the particular requirements and preferences of these target markets.

When determining new target audiences, take into account variables like psychographics, geography, cultural differences, and demography. Knowing the distinctive qualities of every market can help you create focused advertising strategies that will successfully attract and hold the interest of potential clients.

9.2.2 Create a Marketing Strategy Across Channels
Creating a multichannel marketing plan that makes use of both online and offline media is crucial to reaching a wider audience. By doing this, you'll be able to connect with more people and make your brand more noticeable.

You can reach a global audience and produce leads by using online channels including social media, search engine optimization (SEO), email marketing, content marketing, and online advertising. Reaching local or specialty markets can be facilitated by using offline channels like print media, radio, television, and events.

You may increase your reach and impact with a marketing strategy that is cohesive and combines online and offline platforms. In order to maximize your marketing efforts and distribute resources efficiently, don't forget to monitor and evaluate each channel's effectiveness.

9.2.3 Target Your Marketing at the Local Level

Getting into new geographic areas is a common way to increase your market reach. It's critical to localize your marketing initiatives if you want to successfully enter these areas. Localization entails modifying your branding, communication tactics, and marketing messaging to better appeal to the target market's local culture and tastes.

When localizing your marketing efforts, keep things like language, cultural norms, customs, and values in mind. Use imagery and allusions that are culturally appropriate, translate your marketing materials into the local tongue, and modify your content to speak to the unique requirements and preferences of the target market.

Creating a partnership with local businesses, groups, or individuals can also assist you in building trust and credibility in the new market. By exhibiting comprehension and admiration of the regional customs, you can establish trusting bonds with prospective clients and raise your chances of success.

9.2.4 Work together with strategic partners.

Increasing your market reach through strategic partner collaboration can be a successful strategy. Find companies or groups that have a similar target market but provide different but related goods or services. You may reach a larger audience and take advantage of their current client base by collaborating with these organizations.

There are many different ways that strategic alliances can be implemented, including collaborative marketing initiatives, co-branded goods or services, cross-promotions, or referral schemes. Through these partnerships, you can expand into new markets, build brand recognition, and produce leads.

Make sure the mission, values, and brand of any potential strategic partners you are considering match your own. Long-term success can result from a collaboration that benefits both sides and creates a win-win situation.

9.2.5 Make Use of Technology and Online Shopping

The digital age we live in today offers a plethora of chances to reach a wider audience through technology and e-commerce platforms. To expand your audience and boost sales, think about using online markets like Amazon, eBay, or Etsy.

Invest in a visually beautiful, search engine-optimized e-commerce website that is easy to use. This will assist you in gaining organic traffic and converting site visitors into paying clients. To foster loyalty and trust, use secure payment channels and deliver top-notch customer support.

Furthermore, contemplate employing cutting-edge technologies like augmented reality, virtual reality, and artificial intelligence to improve consumer satisfaction and set your company apart from rivals. With the use of these technologies, you can produce engaging and interactive experiences that appeal to your intended audience.

9.2.6: Increase the Range of Goods and Services You Offer
Diversifying your offerings of goods and services is another way to increase the size of your market. Determine what extras you may offer that will appeal to your target market and enhance your current offerings. This can boost client loyalty and help you draw in new business.

To learn about the requirements and preferences of your target market, conduct market research. Make use of this data to create new goods or services that solve their problems or offer value. Make sure the quality and consumer satisfaction of these new offerings are in line with your brand.

You can reach a larger market and meet a greater range of client needs by broadening the range of products or services you offer.

9.2.7 Keep an eye on and adjust to market trends.

It's critical to keep up with market trends and modify your tactics as necessary if you want to increase your market reach. Keep an eye on rival activity, market news, and customer reviews to spot new trends or changes in consumer behavior.

You can proactively modify your product offers, distribution networks, and marketing messaging to conform to shifting market dynamics by staying ahead of the curve. By doing this, you'll be able to keep your advantage over competitors and keep reaching new markets.

In summary

Reaching a wider audience is essential to growing your company and attaining long-term success. You can effectively expand your market reach and increase your customer base by identifying new target markets, creating a multichannel marketing strategy, localizing your marketing efforts, working with strategic partners, utilizing technology and e-commerce, growing your product or service offerings, and keeping an eye on market trends. It is vital to consistently assess and refine your tactics in order to guarantee long-term expansion and financial gain.

9.3 Handling a Rise in Demand

You can encounter a new difficulty if your company takes off and your goods or services become well-liked: handling the surge in demand. For any entrepreneur, this is an exciting time, but if you're unprepared, it may also be intimidating. This section will discuss tactics to help you successfully handle the spike in demand and make sure your company keeps growing.

9.3.1 Streamlining the Way Things Are Done

Streamlining your operations is essential to meeting the expanding needs of your customers as demand for your product or service rises. To increase productivity and efficiency, you must optimize your workflows and processes. You can simplify your operations by following these steps:

Invest in technologies or software that can help you automate repetitive work. Determine which tasks can be automated. You and your staff will have more time, as a result, to concentrate on other important facets of your company.

Put scalable systems in place to make sure your infrastructure and systems are able to meet the additional demand. This could entail enhancing supply chain management, increasing production capacity, or modernizing your technology.

Optimize your inventory management by closely monitoring your stock levels to prevent excess or stockouts. Install inventory management solutions that can automate reordering procedures and offer real-time visibility.

Simplify customer service: Offering top-notch customer service is crucial when your clientele expands. To effectively handle client questions, put in place a ticketing system or customer relationship management (CRM) software.

You can make sure that your company can handle the increasing demand without sacrificing quality or client pleasure by optimizing your operations.

9.3.2 Production Scaling
You might have to boost your production capacity in order to keep up with the demand. This entails growing the quantity of service providers or your manufacturing capabilities. The following tactics will enable you to efficiently scale your production:

Determine how much you can produce right now. Evaluate your present production capacity and note any restrictions or bottlenecks that might make it more difficult for you to grow. This could be due to a lack of space, equipment, or experienced workers.

Invest in technology and equipment: To boost output, if your present capacity for production is inadequate, think about making an investment in new technology or equipment. This could entail investing in new machinery, updating current gear, or putting automated solutions into place.

Consider outsourcing or subcontracting some parts of your production process if you are unable to scale your production internally. By doing this, you may fulfill the rising demand without having to make a large capital expenditure.

Work together with suppliers: cultivate a stronger rapport with suppliers and look into joint venture prospects. This could entail working with suppliers to expand manufacturing capacity, obtaining better rates, or gaining priority access to raw materials.

To guarantee a seamless transition, scaling up production necessitates meticulous preparation and cooperation. You may meet the growing demand for your product or service without sacrificing its quality or consistency by putting these tactics into practice.

9.3.3 Taking Care of the Supply Chain
You must have a strong and stable supply chain

in place as your company expands in order to fulfill the rising demand. The following are some essential factors to take into account when managing your supply chain:

Expand the range of suppliers you work with. Depending too much on one provider can be dangerous, particularly if that supplier can't keep up with demand. To lower the chance of interruptions and guarantee a consistent supply of components or raw materials, diversify your supplier base.

Build trusting and transparent connections with suppliers. Develop trusting and transparent relationships with your suppliers. To make sure they can satisfy your objectives, be sure to regularly convey your production projections and requirements.

Put supply chain visibility into practice by putting in place tools or systems that give you real-time supply chain visibility. This can assist you in spotting possible delays or bottlenecks and taking preventative action to lessen them.

Inventory levels should be closely monitored in order to prevent stockouts and surplus inventory. Install inventory management solutions that can automate reordering procedures and offer real-time visibility.

You can minimize disruptions, fulfill client demand, and maintain a regular flow of goods or components by managing your supply chain correctly.

9.3.4 Recruiting and Education

You might need to bring on more employees as your company expands in order to handle the added workload. Efficient management of growing demand requires hiring the right people and giving them the correct training. Here are some pointers for selecting and onboarding new staff members:

Establish job roles and responsibilities: To make sure that new hires are aware of what is expected of them, clearly outline the duties and responsibilities of each position.

Recruit strategically: Create a hiring plan that is in line with the objectives and core values of your company. To draw in top talent, use a variety of platforms, including social media, job boards, and professional networks.

Conduct in-depth interviews: Give interviews plenty of your time to evaluate candidates' qualifications, backgrounds, and cultural fit. To obtain a variety of viewpoints, think about interviewing important team members.

Give new hires thorough training. After hiring them, make sure they receive thorough training so they have the abilities and information needed to carry out their jobs well. This could entail external training classes, mentorship programs, or on-the-job training.

Building a strong team that can manage the rising demand and support the expansion and success of your company starts with selecting and training the right candidates.

9.3.5 Observation and Input

It's critical to keep an eye on your operations, client feedback, and market developments as you handle growing demand. This will assist you in determining where you need to improve and making the required changes. The following are some methods for keeping an eye on and obtaining feedback:

Put performance metrics into practice by defining key performance indicators (KPIs) that correspond with your company's objectives and by routinely monitoring and evaluating them. This will give you information about how well your operations are performing and assist you in identifying areas that need improvement.

Get feedback from your clients: Ask for feedback from your clients on a regular basis to learn about their requirements, preferences, and degree of satisfaction. You can accomplish this through direct communication, reviews, or surveys.

Keep up with market trends: Pay particular attention to changes in the market, advancements in the industry, and actions taken by competitors. By doing this, you'll be able to remain ahead of the curve and make wise decisions to satisfy your clients' changing wants.

Promote employee feedback: Foster an environment of open communication and encourage staff members to offer comments and ideas for enhancements. They are at the forefront of your company and can offer insightful information.

You can make data-driven decisions, pinpoint areas for development, and make sure your company keeps up with client demands as it grows by keeping an eye on things and soliciting feedback.

For any firm, handling higher demand is an exciting time, but it also presents unique difficulties. You can successfully handle the spike in demand and set up your company for long-term success by optimizing processes, increasing output, controlling the supply chain, selecting and preparing the proper personnel, and regularly monitoring and obtaining feedback.

9.4 Infrastructure and Operational Scaling

The exciting stage of business scaling denotes success and development. It is the process of growing your infrastructure and operations to meet rising demand and penetrate new markets. In order to ensure that your firm can handle the expansion without compromising quality or customer pleasure, scaling effectively involves rigorous planning and execution. We'll go over the main ideas and tactics for growing your infrastructure and operations in this part.

9.4.1 Evaluating Your Present-Day Activities

It's crucial to evaluate your present operations to find any bottlenecks or areas that require improvement before scaling your organization. With the aid of this review, you will gain insight into the advantages and disadvantages of your current infrastructure and procedures. Take into account the following elements:

Capacity: Determine whether your present

processes are able to accommodate a rise in demand. Examine your distribution routes, supply chain, and production capability to see if they can accommodate expansion.

Efficiency: Seek ways to simplify your business processes and get rid of any inefficiencies. Determine the areas where technology or automation can cut expenses and increase productivity.

Scalability: Find out if the infrastructure you have now can grow with your company. Take into account elements like your physical area, equipment, and IT systems. Determine whether they have the capacity to handle more production or service delivery.

Customer Experience: Consider the potential effects of scaling on the customer experience. Will it have an impact on customer service, delivery schedules, or product quality? Make sure that as you grow, the value and satisfaction you offer to your clients are not jeopardized.

9.4.2 Formulating a Plan for Scalability

Having evaluated your present operations, the next step is to create a scalability plan. The actions and tactics you must use in order to successfully scale your firm will be described in this strategy. Take into account the following factors when developing your scalability plan:

Infrastructure: Ascertain what kind of

infrastructure you'll need to grow your business. This could entail buying new equipment, improving your IT infrastructure, or increasing your physical space. Make sure your infrastructure can handle the extra demand without sacrificing the caliber of your goods or services.

Procedures and Systems: Examine your current procedures and systems to find any weaknesses or potential areas for development. Streamline your operations to increase efficiency and lower errors by automating repetitive procedures, putting in place effective workflows, and integrating technologies.

Supply Chain: Assess your supply chain's capacity to meet rising demand. Determine any possible limits or hazards, then create backup measures to lessen them. In order to guarantee a dependable and effective supply chain, think about broadening your supplier base and building solid relationships.

Staffing: Evaluate your present workforce to see if you need to teach current employees to take on more responsibilities or hire more workers. Take into account the knowledge and abilities needed for scaling, and make sure the proper personnel are in place to assist your expansion.

Customer service: Growing your company might bring in more clients and a rise in questions from potential clients. Create a strategy for managing customer service so that you can continue to provide excellent customer service even as your business expands.

9.4.3 Putting Scalability Plans into Practice

Scalability strategy implementation calls for meticulous preparation and carrying out. To efficiently scale your operations and infrastructure, take into account the following strategies:

Standardization: To guarantee efficiency and consistency, standardize your workflows and processes. As your company expands, this will make it simpler to train new hires and maintain quality.

Automation: Streamline your operations by utilizing technology and automation. Use software programs that can handle repetitive jobs like order processing, inventory control, and customer service. Your staff will have more time to devote to more strategic tasks as a result.

Outsourcing: Take into account contracting with outside suppliers or contractors to handle some tasks or procedures. By doing this, you can grow rapidly without having to make large infrastructure investments or hire more employees. Determine which tasks can be successfully outsourced while upholding quality standards.

Cooperation: Seek alliances or joint ventures with

other companies to benefit from their knowledge, assets, or clientele. This can assist you in reaching a wider audience and scaling more effectively.

Continuous Improvement: To find areas for improvement, keep an eye on and assess your operations on a regular basis. To discover pain areas and execute improvements that improve efficiency and customer satisfaction, solicit feedback from both staff and consumers.

9.4.4 Handling the Difficulties of Growing
There are unique obstacles that come with growing your business. A seamless transition must be ensured by being proactive and well-prepared to handle these obstacles. Take into account these suggestions:

Cash Flow Management: Infrastructure, marketing, and employment are upfront costs associated with scaling. Make sure you have a strong cash flow management strategy in place to support these expenditures and keep your company going while it grows.

Training and Development: Make an investment in training and development initiatives to provide your staff members with the abilities and know-how required to take on more responsibility. They will be better able to adjust to the changes and help your expanded operations succeed as a result.

Collaboration and Communication: Throughout the scaling process, keep the lines of communication open with your team. Encourage a cooperative work atmosphere where staff members are at ease discussing ideas and issues. This will assist you in quickly resolving any problems and guaranteeing a seamless transfer.

Sustaining Quality: It's critical to keep your goods and services up to par as you grow. To make sure that your solutions meet or exceed consumer expectations, put quality control procedures in place and evaluate client feedback on a regular basis.

Flexibility and adaptability: Be ready to modify your plans and strategy in response to unanticipated obstacles or shifts in the market. In order to overcome any challenges that may come up along the way, remain nimble and adaptable.

Growing your infrastructure and operations is a thrilling and difficult task. You may grow your company and reach new heights by evaluating your present operations, creating a plan for scalability, putting good methods into practice, and handling obstacles. Remain committed to your vision and objectives, and as you advance, keep coming up with new ideas and evolving.

MANAGING RISKS AND CHALLENGES

10.1 Recognizing Possible Dangers

Although launching a business is an exciting venture, there are hazards involved. It's critical for entrepreneurs to understand these risks and have a strategy in place to reduce them. In this section, we'll look at some typical hazards that business owners encounter and talk about how to recognize and handle them.

10.1.1 Dangers of the Market

Market risk is one of the main hazards that businesses deal with. This alludes to the potential that there might not be sufficient market demand for your good or service. Before starting your firm, it's critical to carry out in-depth market research in order to detect potential dangers.

Determine who your target audience is and get familiar with their requirements and preferences first. This will assist you in figuring out whether there is a market for your goods or services. Furthermore, examine the competitors to determine whether the market already has comparable products. Gaining market share could be difficult in a highly competitive environment.

Think about running a pilot test or releasing a minimum viable product (MVP) to see whether there is consumer demand and get feedback in order to reduce market risk. This will enable you to make the required modifications prior to making a complete investment in your company.

10.1.2 Hazards Related to Money

Another major concern for entrepreneurs is financial risk. It takes money to start a business, and there's always a danger that you won't make enough money to pay your bills or return debts. Making a thorough financial plan is essential to identifying possible financial dangers.

Estimate your first and continuing costs first. Take into account elements like salaries, marketing, rent, utilities, and inventory. Next, project your revenue using sales projections and market research. This will assist you in assessing the financial viability of your enterprise.

Investigate several funding sources, including crowdsourcing, grant and loan applications, investor searches, bootstrapping, and grant applications, to reduce financial risk. It's also critical to have a backup plan in place in the event that financial difficulties arise for your company. This can entail finding new financing sources, renegotiating contracts, or making cost reductions.

10.1.3 Danger to Operations

Operational risk is the term used to describe the possible difficulties or disruptions that could occur during regular corporate operations. This can involve problems like equipment breakdowns, personnel turnover, and interruptions in the supply chain. It is crucial to carry out an exhaustive evaluation of your company's operations in order to pinpoint possible operational hazards.

Determine the crucial dependencies and processes first. This entails being aware of your production procedures, supplier chain, and key employees. Evaluate the possible consequences of any disturbances to these procedures and create backup measures to lessen the hazards.

Diversifying your supply chain, purchasing backup equipment, and putting in place comprehensive personnel training and retention programs are all good ways to reduce operational risk. To find opportunities for improvement and reduce hazards, it's also critical to periodically assess and update your operational procedures.

10.1.4 Dangers from Law and Regulation
The possible legal and compliance problems that your company can encounter are referred to as legal and regulatory risks. This can involve problems like lawsuits, breaking industry rules, or intellectual property violations. It's critical to speak with legal experts and keep up-to-date on pertinent laws and regulations in order to recognize any legal and regulatory issues.

To begin with, thoroughly examine your company's operations to find any possible legal or compliance concerns. This could involve filing patents, doing trademark searches, or making sure that rules particular to a given industry are followed. Establishing appropriate contracts and agreements is crucial for safeguarding your company's interests.

Collaborate closely with legal experts to guarantee adherence to all relevant laws and regulations in order to reduce legal and regulatory risk. Review and update your contracts and legal papers on a regular basis to take into account any modifications to the law. Additionally, to shield your company from potential liabilities, think about getting the right insurance coverage.

10.1.5 Dangers to Reputation

Reputational risk is the possibility of harming the standing of your company. This could happen as a result of unethical company tactics, subpar products, or bad customer experiences. It's critical to actively monitor and manage the reputation of your brand in order to spot any reputational hazards.

Begin by keeping a frequent eye on reviews and comments from customers. Social media, internet platforms, and client surveys can all be used for this. Respond quickly to any unfavorable comments and take action to fix any problems raised by customers. Make sure your goods and services constantly fulfill or exceed the expectations of your clients.

Concentrate on creating a distinctive brand identity and providing outstanding customer service to reduce reputational risk. Establish strong quality control procedures to guarantee a constant level of quality in your goods or services. A crisis management strategy should be in place in order to swiftly and efficiently handle any possible reputational problems.

The effect that certain hazards may have on your company can be reduced by recognizing them and creating plans to reduce them. Keep in mind that risk management is a continuous process, and as your company grows, it's critical to periodically assess and update your risk mitigation plans.

10.2 Formulating Techniques for Risk Mitigation

Taking chances is part of starting a business. Although risks are unavoidable, it is essential to create efficient risk mitigation plans in order to reduce any potential harm to your company. In order to secure the long-term viability of your endeavor, we shall examine several risk identification and management techniques in this part.

10.2.1 Recognizing Possible Dangers

Identification of possible risks is a prerequisite for developing risk mitigation strategies for your firm. The following are some typical hazards that business owners face:

Market Risk: The success of your firm may be impacted by shifts in consumer tastes, market demand, or economic circumstances. It's critical to keep abreast of market developments and prepare for any changes.

Financial Risk: Your company may be exposed to financial risk due to inadequate cash flow, unforeseen costs, or downturns in the economy. To reduce these risks, make careful financial plans and keep a close eye on your financial situation.

Operational Risk: Problems with technology, the supply chain, or production could cause disruptions in your business. Establish reliable operational procedures, keep backup systems up-to-date, and routinely check for vulnerabilities.

Legal and Regulatory Risk: Violations of laws and regulations may give rise to legal issues as well as harm to your reputation. Make sure your company is operating within the law by keeping up with pertinent laws and regulations.

Competitive Risk: Your market share may be impacted by rivals joining the market or providing comparable goods or services. Keep an eye on the market competition and set your company apart with unique products and first-rate customer service.

Human Resources Risk: The productivity and culture of your company may be impacted by internal disagreements, employee turnover, or a shortage of trained workers. Establish productive hiring and retention techniques, cultivate a happy workplace, and make training investments for staff members.

Technological Risk: Your products or services may become outdated due to the rapid improvements in technology. To stay ahead of the curve, keep up with technical advancements, make research and development investments, and welcome innovation,.

10.2.2 Formulating Strategies for Risk Mitigation
It's time to create methods to reduce potential hazards once you've identified them. Here are a few practical risk-reduction techniques to think about:

Diversification: By expanding your target markets or range of products and services, you can lessen the impact of market risk. You can reduce the risk of depending too much on a single market by serving a variety of clientele or sectors.

Financial Planning and Contingency Funds: Create a thorough financial plan that takes risk assessment, budgeting, and forecasting into account. Set up emergency funds to cover unforeseen costs or decreases in revenue.

Insurance: Invest in the right insurance coverage to safeguard your company against future threats. To determine which insurance policies, such as property, liability, or business interruption insurance, best meet your company's needs, speak with insurance experts.

Contractual Agreements: Make sure you have carefully established contracts in place before getting into any partnerships, collaborations, or supplier agreements. To reduce operational and legal risks, clearly identify roles, duties, and conflict resolution procedures.

Frequent Monitoring and Assessment: Keep an eye on the health of your company's operations, industry developments, and possible threats. To detect new hazards and take preventative action, use key performance indicators (KPIs) and routine risk assessments.

Developing Strong Relationships: Take care of your connections with vendors, clients, and other stakeholders. By working together and pooling resources, strong partnerships can reduce risks and offer support during trying times.

Cybersecurity Measures: It's critical to safeguard

your company against cyber dangers in the current digital era. To protect sensitive data for your company, put strong cybersecurity measures in place, such as firewalls, encryption, and frequent data backups.

Crisis Management Plan: Create a thorough crisis management plan that specifies actions to be performed in case of an unforeseen difficulty or crisis. To reduce disruptions, this strategy should contain alternate operational methods, communication techniques, and backup plans.

10.2.3 Overcoming Unexpected Obstacles
In the course of your entrepreneurial endeavors, unforeseen obstacles could appear despite your best efforts. The following are some methods for overcoming these obstacles:

Remain Calm and Flexible: When confronted with unforeseen obstacles, keep a composed and adaptable attitude. Resilience and adaptability are essential qualities of prosperous businesspeople.

Seek Expert Advice: Don't be afraid to approach business consultants, mentors, or professionals in the field. Their knowledge and perceptions might offer helpful direction while negotiating difficult circumstances.

Work together and establish a strong network of experts and entrepreneurs that can provide support and direction when things get tough. Work together to pool resources and come up with creative solutions.

Learn from Mistakes: See obstacles as chances to gain knowledge. Examine the circumstances, determine what has to be done better, and make the necessary adjustments to avoid reoccurring problems.

10.2.4 Acknowledging Setbacks and Rebounding
An inevitable aspect of becoming an entrepreneur is failure. Accepting failure as a teaching moment and utilizing it as a springboard for achievement is crucial. The following are some strategies for overcoming setbacks and growing:

Think and Examine: Give the causes of the failure some thought. Examine what went wrong, determine the lessons that were learned, and apply this understanding to your next initiatives to make them better.

Adapt and develop: Make use of the knowledge that comes from mistakes to both develop and modify your business plan. Accept change and always look for methods to make your goods, services, or procedures better.

Seek Support: Put yourself in the company of peers, mentors, or business coaches who can offer support and direction when things get tough. Their viewpoints and experiences can help you overcome obstacles.

Remain Persistent: Recall that failing is not a sign

of failure but rather a chance to learn and advance. Remain optimistic and tenacious in your pursuit of your objectives.

You can confidently navigate the risks and challenges of entrepreneurship by creating efficient risk mitigation measures, handling unforeseen obstacles, and learning from mistakes. Recall that all prosperous entrepreneurs have encountered challenges during their journey; what distinguishes them is their capacity for adaptation and tenacity.

10.3 Overcoming Unexpected Obstacles

Establishing and maintaining a business is not always easy. Unexpected obstacles will inevitably arise while you transform your concept into a profitable company. These difficulties could be anything from small failures to significant roadblocks that jeopardize your company's continued survival. You can overcome these obstacles and emerge stronger on the other side, though, if you have the appropriate attitude and coping mechanisms.

10.3.1 Adopting a Growth Mentality

It's critical to have a growth mindset when dealing

with unforeseen obstacles. The idea that you can learn and develop from every circumstance, even if it first appears to be a failure or setback, is known as a growth mindset. Consider difficulties as chances for development and progress rather than obstacles to overcome. Accept that obstacles are a normal part of the business path and that you are capable of overcoming them.

10.3.2 Determining the Primary Cause

Finding the source of an issue is essential when unforeseen difficulties emerge. Analyze the circumstances and determine what caused the challenge. This will assist you in creating workable plans to deal with the problem and keep it from happening again later on. Finding the underlying cause of the issue will enable you to address it head-on and provide sustainable solutions.

10.3.3 Looking for assistance and knowledge

You don't have to confront unforeseen difficulties by yourself. Consult with mentors, advisors, or other business owners who have gone through comparable struggles for support and direction. Their knowledge and experience can offer insightful viewpoints and support you in resolving challenging circumstances. In addition, think about becoming a member of networking or entrepreneurial organizations where you can meet people who share your interests and receive guidance and assistance.

10.3.4 Formulating Backup Plans

Having backup plans in place is one of the best strategies to handle unforeseen obstacles. Plan ahead for possible hazards and create solutions to reduce them. This could entail setting up backup sources, expanding your clientele, or setting aside money for unexpected expenses. By anticipating problems before they arise, you may lessen their effects and make sure that business operations can go on as usual.

10.3.5 Keeping an Upbeat Attitude

It's critical to keep a positive outlook when faced with unforeseen difficulties. When plans don't work out, it's easy to feel overwhelmed or demoralized. On the other hand, an optimistic outlook might support your motivation and solution-finding concentration. Recall that every obstacle offers a chance for development and progress and that setbacks are only temporary. If you want to keep your attitude resilient, surround yourself with supportive people and take care of yourself.

10.3.6 Taking Lessons from Mistakes

Entrepreneurship inevitably involves failure, and failure is frequently accompanied by unforeseen difficulties. Consider failure a valuable learning experience rather than a bad result. Spend some time thinking back on what went wrong and figuring out what you can learn from it. Take failure as a chance to hone your tactics, enhance your ability to make decisions, and develop as a business owner. Recall that many prosperous businesspeople had setbacks prior to attaining their final accomplishment.

10.3.7 Creating and Modifying

Unexpected obstacles may require you to modify and creatively approach your business plan. Be flexible and eager to try out novel strategies. This can entail changing the direction of your product or service, looking into untapped markets, or identifying different sources of income. Accepting change and being open to adapting will help you get past unforeseen obstacles and set up your company for long-term success.

10.3.8 Strengthening Resilience

The capacity to overcome obstacles and setbacks is resilience. It is an essential quality for business owners, particularly in the face of unforeseen challenges. Building resilience entails self-care, coping mechanism development, and maintaining a solid support system. Make sure you look after your physical and emotional health, ask for assistance when you need it, and surround yourself with supportive people. By developing resilience, you'll be able to face unforeseen obstacles head-on and persevere.

10.3.9 Honoring Little Victories

While facing unforeseen obstacles, it's critical to acknowledge and appreciate little victories along the way. Even if it appears small in comparison to the difficulties you are facing, recognize and celebrate the progress you have achieved. Honoring modest victories can inspire you, raise your spirits, and serve as a reminder of the good things that have happened along your business path. No matter how minor the accomplishment, take the time to recognize it and use it as motivation to keep going.

10.3.10: Getting Expert Assistance

Unexpected difficulties may call for expert assistance. Don't be afraid to ask experts in the industry for help if you need legal counsel, financial guidance, or specific information. They may offer direction and assistance to help you get through difficult situations and make sure your company keeps moving forward. Recall that asking for assistance is a sign of strength rather than weakness.

Overcoming unforeseen obstacles is an essential aspect of becoming an entrepreneur. You may get through these obstacles and keep moving toward realizing your dream career by adopting a development mindset, getting help, and coming up with practical solutions. Never forget that every obstacle presents a chance for development and education. Remain strong, maintain your optimism, and keep moving forward.

10.4 Acknowledging Setbacks and Rebounding

A necessary component of every entrepreneurial endeavor is failure. The question is not if you will fail, but rather when. Failure, though, shouldn't be viewed as the end of the path. As a matter of fact, it might be an advantageous educational opportunity that helps you succeed. This part will discuss the value of growing from mistakes and how to overcome them to become stronger than before.

10.4.1 Seeing Failure as a Chance to Learn

Many people have a negative perception of failure and believe it should be avoided at all costs. Nonetheless, prosperous businesspeople are aware that failure is a necessary component of learning. It offers insightful information and lessons that can advance and develop you. Rather than being afraid of failing, see it as a chance to grow and change.

When you experience failure, give yourself

some time to consider what went wrong and why. Determine the elements that contributed to the failure by doing an unbiased analysis of the circumstances. You will have a better understanding of your strengths and shortcomings, as well as the areas in which you still need to grow, by doing this self-reflection.

10.4.2 Taking Lessons from Errors

Errors are unavoidable, particularly when launching a new company. The secret is to see errors as opportunities rather than obstacles on the path to achievement. Every error is a chance for growth and learning. You can keep from making the same mistakes again by admitting to them and taking lessons from them.

Maintaining a journal or experience record is a useful strategy for learning from your errors. Keep a record of your errors, the knowledge you gained, and the adjustments you made as a result. You will find this to be a useful resource that you can use later on.

10.4.3 Asking for Opinions and Counsel

Getting input and counsel from others is a crucial part of learning from mistakes. Assemble a network of fellow entrepreneurs, mentors, and advisers who can offer insightful advice. Their viewpoints can give you a new perspective on your mistakes and offer insightful guidance on how to move past them.

Never hesitate to request feedback from your clientele. Their feedback can offer insightful explanations of what went wrong and suggestions for improvement. Utilize this feedback to iterate on your product or service and make the necessary changes.

10.4.4 Building Perseverance and Resilience

Although failing can be demoralizing, it's crucial to cultivate resiliency and persistence. Entrepreneurs who are successful recognize that obstacles are fleeting and that numerous failures are frequently followed by success. Reject failure as a motivator to keep going and never give up on your goals.

Positivity and the capacity to learn from mistakes are essential for building resilience and perseverance. Assemble a network of friends, family, and other business owners who will support you and provide you with motivation and encouragement when things get tough. Recall that failure is a chance to learn and grow, rather than a reflection of your value or skill.

10.4.5 Rejoicing in Little Victories

Even though failure is a necessary part of becoming an entrepreneur, it's crucial to recognize and appreciate little victories along the way. Acknowledge and celebrate your accomplishments, regardless of how minor they may appear. Honoring modest victories raises spirits and gives one more reason to press on.

You may foster a helpful and upbeat atmosphere that promotes development and advancement by acknowledging little victories. It also aids in keeping perspective and equilibrium by serving as a constant reminder that success is a process rather than a destination.

10.4.6 Remaining Flexible and Steady

It's critical to maintain your flexibility and adaptability when facing failure. Since the corporate environment is always changing, being able to change course and adapt is essential for long-term success. Reevaluate your company plan and make the required changes in light of any setbacks.

Be willing to take measured risks and maintain an open mind to new concepts. Accept change and be prepared to part with concepts or tactics that aren't working. You can navigate through failure and come out stronger and more resilient if you continue to be flexible and adaptive.

10.4.7 Taking a Cue from Prosperous Business Owners

Examining prosperous businesspeople who have confronted and conquered comparable obstacles is one of the finest methods to learn from failure. Consume literature, tune in to podcasts, and go to conferences where accomplished businesspeople recount their experiences. Take what you can from their path and incorporate their tactics into your own.

Entrepreneurs who are successful frequently have a lot of information and wisdom to provide. You can steer clear of typical traps and quicken your own journey to success by taking lessons from their mistakes and accomplishments.

10.4.8 Going Forward with Self-Assuredness
Failure is just a detour on the route to success, not the conclusion of the journey. You may recover from failure more powerfully than ever by seeing it as a teaching opportunity, asking for help and advice, growing in fortitude and tenacity, appreciating little victories, remaining flexible and nimble, and taking lessons from prosperous business owners.

Recall that the most prosperous businesspeople had to overcome numerous setbacks before realizing their goals. Continue onward with confidence, using setbacks as stepping stones to victory. Failing along the way is only part of the route to your ideal job.

MAINTAINING WORK-LIFE BALANCE

11.1 Establishing Limits and Prioritizing

It's easy for an aspirant business owner to become engrossed in the thrill and enthusiasm of creating their ideal enterprise. Setting limits and wisely allocating your time and energy are essential, though. If you don't set clear boundaries and prioritize your tasks, you can end up feeling overburdened, anxious, and unable to strike a healthy work-life balance.

11.1.1 Establishing Your Limits

Establishing boundaries is crucial to maintaining a distinct division between your personal and professional lives. Without boundaries, it's easy to allow work to take up all of your time, which can cause burnout and strained relationships. The following techniques will assist you in setting and upholding boundaries:

Set aside particular hours to work on your business. Choose times when you will just work on your business. Share these hours with your loved ones, clients, and team so they know when you're available and when you need time to work alone.

Establish a physical area where you may work without interruptions by designating a workplace. This could be a coffee shop, co-working place, or home office. It's easier to mentally keep work and home life apart when you have a designated workspace.

Establish clear guidelines for people to follow. Share your expectations and boundaries with your loved ones, clients, and team. Inform them of your availability and when you need time alone to concentrate on your work. To prevent miscommunications and disputes, promote honest and open communication.

Say no. It's critical to acknowledge your boundaries and refrain from taking on more than you can handle. Refusing opportunities or activities that conflict with your principles or priorities frees up your time to concentrate on the things that are actually important for your company's development.

11.1.2 Setting Task Priorities

Setting boundaries and prioritizing tasks well are essential for successful time and energy management. You may make sure that you are concentrating on the most significant and impactful tasks by setting priorities for your tasks. The following techniques will assist you in setting priorities:

Determine your objectives. Clearly state your company's short- and long-term objectives. This will provide you with a structure for setting priorities for the tasks that will help you achieve your goals.

Divide big jobs into smaller, more manageable pieces. Although big projects can be intimidating, they are easier to do when broken down into smaller chores. Sort these smaller jobs into priorities according to their significance and urgency.

Employ time management strategies: To assist you in setting priorities and managing your time, try out some time management strategies like the Eisenhower Matrix or the Pomodoro Technique.

Concentrate on high-value tasks: Determine which tasks are most important to the success of your company and rank them appropriately. Strategic planning, establishing connections with important stakeholders, and revenue-generating chores are a few examples of these high-value activities.

Acknowledge that you are not able to accomplish everything alone and delegate or outsource. Assign duties that can be completed by others to free up your time so you may concentrate on higher-priority projects. Think about outsourcing jobs that fall outside of your area of expertise or that can be completed more quickly by other experts.

11.1.3 Juggling Professional and Personal Life
It is essential for your general well-being and the long-term viability of your firm to maintain a healthy work-life balance. The following tactics can assist you in striking a long-term work-life balance:

Schedule personal time: Be sure to set aside time for personal pursuits and self-care, just as you would for work-related duties. This could be relaxing, exercising, engaging in hobbies, or just spending time with loved ones. As with any other critical work, prioritize your personal time and treat it as non-negotiable.

Engage in self-care: Make time each day for self-care activities to maintain your physical and emotional health. This could be doing things that make you happy and relaxed, including working out, journaling, or practicing meditation. Making self-care a priority aids in mental renewal and upkeep.

Set boundaries when using technology. With laptops and cellphones, it's easy to stay connected to the office round-the-clock in the modern digital era. Set limits with technology by setting out specified periods of time to unplug gadgets used for work. This frees you from work-related distractions so you may completely participate in personal activities.

Seek assistance: Assemble a network of friends, family, and other business owners who are aware of the difficulties you encounter. Rely on them for counsel, inspiration, and emotional support. Additionally, to manage the challenges of entrepreneurship and preserve a positive work-life balance, think about getting expert assistance, such as counseling or coaching.

Recall that preserving a work-life balance necessitates constant assessment and modification. Your priorities and limits will change as your business does. Make sure you are establishing a sustainable work-life balance that promotes your personal and professional progress by regularly evaluating and improving your strategy.

11.2 Handling Burnout and Stress

It can be thrilling and satisfying to launch and manage your own company, but it can also be quite taxing and stressful. As an entrepreneur, you might have to put in a lot of overtime, deal with ongoing difficulties, and bear the weight of having your company succeed. If not adequately handled, this can quickly result in stress and burnout. We'll look at ways to help you avoid burnout and properly manage stress in this section so you can keep a good work-life balance.

11.2.1 Identifying Stress and Burnout Symptoms
There are several physical and emotional manifestations of stress and burnout. It's critical to recognize the warning signs so you can act before the situation gets out of control. Here are a few typical indicators of stress and burnout:

physical signs such as headaches, exhaustion, and trouble falling asleep.
emotional signs such as anxiety, anger, and despondency.
Reduced efficiency and trouble focusing.

loss of drive or enthusiasm for your work.
withdrawal from relationships and social interactions.
It's critical to take immediate action to address any indicators of these in order to stop more harm from being done to your business and well-being.

11.2.2 Stress-Reduction Techniques

Put self-care first: Taking care of oneself ought to come first. A healthy diet, frequent exercise, and adequate sleep are all important. By engaging in these activities, you'll be able to preserve your mental and physical health and manage stress more effectively.

Use relaxation and mindfulness techniques. Include mindfulness and deep breathing exercises in your everyday practice. This can involve practices like yoga, deep breathing techniques, or meditation. These techniques can aid in lowering stress levels and encouraging serenity and clarity.

Delegate and Outsource: It's critical for business owners to understand that they are unable to handle every task in-house. Assign work to your team members, or think about contracting out specific duties. By doing this, you'll be able to focus on more important areas of your organization and reduce some of the workload.

Realistic Expectations: Steer clear of having irrational expectations for your company and yourself. Recognize that obstacles and failures are inevitable and that it's acceptable to seek assistance or modify your objectives as needed. Realistic expectations will help you avoid undue strain and tension.

Take Regular Breaks and Time Off: In order to refuel, it's critical to plan time off and take regular breaks throughout the day. Taking a break from work enables you to recover and rest, which will ultimately boost your output and inventiveness when you return.

11.2.3 Avoiding Fatigue

Set Limits: Define distinct boundaries for your personal and professional lives. Establish defined work hours and try your best to adhere to them. Do not answer business calls or check work emails during your personal time. Setting limits will help you keep a better work-life balance.

Seek Support: Assemble a network of friends, family, and other business owners who are aware of the difficulties you encounter. Talk about your experiences, ask for guidance, and rely on them for help when you need it. Sometimes, all it takes to reduce stress is to simply talk about your worries.

Practice time management: Preventing burnout requires effective time management. Set realistic deadlines, prioritize your responsibilities, and refrain from taking on more than you can do. When it's essential, practice saying no and concentrate on activities that support your values and aspirations.

Celebrate Little Wins: Regardless of how minor they may appear, take pride in and acknowledge your accomplishments. Acknowledging your accomplishments and improvements along the way helps keep you motivated and helps you avoid burnout.

11.2.4 Getting Expert Assistance

Seeking professional help may be helpful if stress and burnout are having a severe negative influence on your well-being and capacity to perform. A therapist or counselor can help with stress management and coping strategy development. Never be afraid to ask for assistance when you need it.

Recall that preventing burnout and managing stress are continuous processes. Self-awareness, self-care, and a dedication to upholding a positive work-life balance are necessary. You can successfully manage stress, avoid burnout, and keep moving forward with your goal of landing your ideal job by putting these ideas into practice.

11.3 Seeking Assistance and Obtaining Support
Establishing and maintaining a business can be difficult and sometimes daunting. It's critical to keep in mind that you're not experiencing this alone. Your entrepreneurial experience may significantly change if you ask for and get support. We'll look at a number of strategies for getting support and assistance while you work through the highs and lows of landing your ideal job in this part.

11.3.1 Connecting with Networks and Communities of Entrepreneurs
Connecting with entrepreneurial communities and networks is one of the finest methods to ask for and get support. These communities give like-minded people a place to interact, exchange stories, and give advice. They could be a great source of motivation, guidance, and encouragement.

Numerous offline and online networks and communities are tailored especially for business owners. Through online resources like LinkedIn,

Facebook groups, and industry-specific forums, you can network with other business owners, exchange questions, and gain knowledge from their experiences. Meeting fellow entrepreneurs face-to-face and forming deep connections are made possible by offline networks like local business associations and networking gatherings.

It is crucial to actively participate in and contribute to these groups once you join them. Ask questions, provide others with encouragement, and share your own experiences. Participating in the community can help you build relationships that may result in collaborations, partnerships, and mentorship possibilities, in addition to providing you with insightful advice.

11.3.2 Looking for a Mentor

A useful tool for both professional and personal development is mentoring. A mentor is a person with experience and knowledge in your field or sector who may offer direction, assistance, and advice. They can support you in overcoming obstacles, choosing wisely, and staying clear of typical traps.

Acquiring a mentor might significantly alter your entrepreneurial path. Find people who have succeeded in the field you want to work in or who are knowledgeable in the areas you need help with. Make contact with them and convey your desire to gain knowledge from their experiences. Show them that you appreciate their time and explain how both of you may benefit from their mentoring.

Group mentorship programs, virtual check-ins, one-on-one meetings, and other formats are all possible for mentoring. Building a relationship based on open communication, mutual respect, and trust is crucial. Keep in mind that mentoring is a two-way street, and you should be prepared to give back and enrich the partnership as well.

11.3.3 Employing Specialists and Professionals

You can encounter difficulties and assignments outside of your area of competence as an entrepreneur. In situations like these, getting assistance from specialists and professionals can help you avoid wasting time, money, or stress. Hiring professionals can offer the particular knowledge and abilities required to overcome challenges and advance your organization, whether it's legal guidance, accounting services, marketing expertise, or technical help.

It's crucial to perform due diligence when hiring specialists and look for people or companies with a track record of success and suitable experience. To be sure it's a good fit, study reviews, ask around for suggestions from reliable people, and set up interviews. Keep in mind that investing in professional recruiting is an investment in the success of your company, so value competence and quality over price.

11.3.4 Establishing a Helpful Network

Having a strong support system of friends, family, and coworkers can help you stay motivated when things get tough, in addition to joining business communities and looking for guidance. Your entrepreneurial path can be greatly impacted by surrounding yourself with positive, like-minded people who share your vision.

Inform your network of supporters of your goals and aspirations and provide them with regular updates on your advancement. Together, celebrate your accomplishments and rely on one another for support when things go wrong. Having a solid support network may keep you resilient, driven, and focused when faced with challenges.

11.3.5 Making Personal Development Invested

Finally, requesting assistance and support can only be achieved by making an investment in your own personal growth. In addition to strengthening your entrepreneurial abilities, ongoing study and skill development can lead to new connections and opportunities.

Think about going to conferences, seminars, and workshops in your field or interests. These gatherings offer beneficial networking and educational possibilities. Reading books, listening to podcasts, and following influential people in your industry can also help you learn new things and broaden your horizons.

Recall that the pursuit of personal growth is a continuous process. Adopt a growth mentality and show yourself to be receptive to new information. By making an investment in yourself, you'll not only improve as an entrepreneur but also draw in support and assistance from people who value your dedication to both professional and personal development.

In summary

Seeking assistance and support is crucial to making your ideal career a reality. These tactics, which include investing in personal growth, hiring professionals, networking with like-minded individuals, joining entrepreneurial organizations, and looking for mentorship, can offer the support, motivation, and know-how required to overcome obstacles and succeed. Recall that you are not alone on the entrepreneurial path. Accept the strength of support and ask for assistance when required.

11.4 Establishing Long-Term Work-Life Harmony

Establishing a long-term work-life equilibrium is essential for company owners and entrepreneurs. It is easy to become engrossed in the thrills and pressures of creating a profitable company, but putting your personal life last can cause burnout and have a detrimental effect on your general health. This section will provide tactics and advice to help you pursue your ideal career while maintaining a healthy work-life balance.

11.4.1 Setting Your Time and Energy Priorities

Setting wise time and energy priorities is one of the first steps towards achieving a long-term work-life balance. It's normal for entrepreneurs to believe that there aren't enough hours in the day to get everything done. You can make sure that you are allocating time for both your personal and professional lives, though, by establishing clear limits and priorities.

Determine what your top daily priorities are and how you want to achieve them. Prioritize doing these jobs before tackling the less important ones. Setting priorities for your job will help you stay on task and move closer to your company's objectives.

Establishing defined work hours and boundaries is also crucial. Working nonstop may seem appealing, but it can rapidly result in burnout. Establish your peak productivity periods and plan your work hours accordingly. Share these boundaries with your clients and team so they know when you need time for yourself and when you are available.

11.4.2 Establishing a Helpful Environment
Creating a welcoming atmosphere is essential to preserving a long-term work-life balance. Your general well-being can be greatly improved by surrounding yourself with others who recognize and value your need for balance.

Ask your friends and relatives for help. Tell them about your objectives and difficulties, as well as how they can help. Having a solid support network can help you stay motivated and offer emotional support when things get hard.

Joining a community or networking group of like-minded business owners is another option to think about. These groups can offer insightful opinions, counsel, and encouragement from people who have gone through comparable struggles. You can maintain a healthy work-life balance while navigating the ups and downs of entrepreneurship by exchanging experiences and learning from others.

11.4.3 Taking Care of Oneself

A long-term work-life balance depends on you taking care of yourself. When you are focused on growing your business, it can be easy to overlook your physical and emotional health, but doing so can have long-term effects.

Schedule time for things that will help you feel refreshed and renewed. This could involve engaging in hobbies and interests outside of work, exercising, practicing meditation, or spending time in nature. Making self-care a priority boosts your creativity and productivity, in addition to your general well-being.

Establishing boundaries between one's personal and professional lives is equally essential. Don't answer business calls or check work emails during your allotted personal time. By unplugging from work, you may rejuvenate and give your whole attention to your personal life, enhancing your relationships and well-being.

11.4.4 Outsourcing and Delegation

It is more crucial than ever to assign work and contract out some duties as your company expands. Doing everything by yourself might result in overwhelm and make it difficult to maintain a healthy work-life balance.

Determine which jobs can be assigned to the members of your team or to outside experts. Accounting, marketing, and administrative work may fall into this category. You can free up time to concentrate on high-value work and spend more time on your personal life by delegating these duties.

When assigning tasks, make sure you provide your team members or contracted experts with precise instructions and expectations. Maintain regular contact and offer constructive criticism to guarantee that assignments are finished to your satisfaction. You'll reduce your workload and create a happier workplace by putting your trust in your team and letting them take responsibility for their tasks.

11.4.5 Having Reasonably High Standards

A sustainable work-life balance depends on having reasonable expectations. Realizing that creating a successful business requires time and work is crucial. Refrain from placing undue pressure on yourself to succeed right away.

Establish attainable objectives and benchmarks for your company, and acknowledge your progress along the way. Accept that obstacles and setbacks are inevitable, but see them as chances for development and education. Setting reasonable goals will help you stay stress-free and have a better work-life balance.

Recall that striking a lasting work-life balance requires constant effort. It necessitates ongoing assessment and modification as your personal and professional lives change. You may pursue your ideal profession and maintain a healthy work-life balance by prioritizing your time and energy, setting reasonable expectations, cultivating a supportive workplace, practicing self-care, outsourcing and delegating, and exercising self-care.

Conclusion

12.1 Taking Stock of Your Travels

Best wishes! Now that you've reached the end of the book, take some time to consider how your idea became a successful venture. You have gained insightful knowledge and useful tactics from this book to help you land your ideal career. It's time to reflect on your progress and take a minute to look back.

12.1.1 Taking the Process to Heart

Establishing a profitable company takes time and effort. It calls for commitment, tenacity, and a readiness to change and grow as you go. You may appreciate the process and recognize your development by looking back on your journey. Keep in mind that every step you've taken, no matter how tiny, has helped you get your ideal career.

12.1.2 Acknowledging Your Triumphs

Let's pause to acknowledge and appreciate our achievements. Examine the objectives you established in your business strategy and note the accomplishments of key milestones. Every success you achieve, whether it's getting finance, starting a profitable marketing initiative, or reaching a wider audience, is a result of your diligence and perseverance.

12.1.3 Taking Lessons from Difficulties

Recognizing the difficulties you have encountered is another aspect of looking back on your trip. There are challenges involved with starting a firm, and it's critical to acknowledge the lessons that may be drawn from them. Think back to the difficulties you faced and the means by which you overcame them. Which tactics did you apply? Which abilities did you acquire? Make the most of these insights to advance as an entrepreneur.

12.1.4 Expressing Thanks and Recognition

Thank you to the folks who have helped and encouraged you along the way. Your success has been greatly influenced by the support and advice of your family, friends, mentors, and team members. Give them a sincere thank you for their assistance and acknowledge the teamwork that has gotten you this far.

12.1.5 Assessing Your Development

Evaluating your professional and personal development is another aspect of reflecting on your trip. Take into consideration your newly obtained abilities, information, and insights. How have you developed as a business owner? In what ways have you improved? Being aware of your progress enables you to keep changing and adapting as you go.

12.1.6 Creating New Objectives

It is imperative that you make new goals for the future as you consider your trip. What comes next now that you have your ideal job? Think about the direction you want to take your company and the new challenges you want to take on. Establish challenging yet doable objectives that will inspire you to succeed and stay motivated.

12.1.7 Motivating Advice

Your journey from concept to success is about encouraging others to follow their ambitions as much as it is about personal accomplishment. Tell prospective business owners about your experience, and provide advice and encouragement to others who are just beginning their own ventures. You may help others and support the entrepreneurial community by sharing your experiences and lessons learned.

12.1.8: Never Stop Learning and Developing

And lastly, keep in mind that the adventure is far from over. Establishing a profitable company is a lifelong process that calls for constant learning and development. Continue to be inquisitive, look for fresh chances, and welcome change. Keeping up with the latest developments is crucial in the ever-changing corporate scene. Make a commitment to continuous education and flexibility in order to secure your ideal career in the long run.

In summary

In summary, one of the most important steps in transforming your day job into your ideal career is to reflect on your experience. It enables you to recognize your successes, draw lessons from setbacks, and make new plans for the future. You can develop as an entrepreneur further by accepting the process, acknowledging your progress, and motivating others. Recall that success is an ongoing process of invention and advancement rather than a destination. I wish you continued success and growth in your ideal job. Congratulations on your accomplishments.

12.2 Honoring Your Achievements

Best wishes! You've been successful in making your ideal career a reality. You have built a strong team, overcome many challenges, validated your idea, validated your business plan, built a prototype, obtained funding, executed successful marketing strategies, scaled your business, managed risks and challenges, and maintained a healthy work-life balance. It's time to acknowledge your accomplishments and take stock of your path.

12.2.1 Celebrate Your Success

Give yourself a moment of thanks for all the hard work and dedication you have put into achieving your ideal job. Celebrate your accomplishments along the way, whether it was landing your first client, hitting a sales goal, or introducing a brand-new good or service. Acknowledge your accomplishments and the effects you have had on the market, your staff, and your clients.

12.2.2 Discuss Your Achievements

Tell people about your accomplishments. Inform your mentors, family, and friends of your accomplishments and growth. Join them in celebrating and thanking them for all of their help and inspiration along the way. Others may be encouraged and inspired by your success story to follow their goals and develop their ideas into profitable ventures.

12.2.3 Give yourself a treat.

Give yourself a reward for your efforts and achievements. Whether it's a spa day, a new device, or a trip, treat yourself to something wonderful. Honor your accomplishments and treat yourself to some well-earned relaxation. Maintaining your passion and drive while you expand and change your business will be made easier by taking the time to rest and recover.

12.2.4 Show Your Team Some Love

Your accomplishments are not the only result of your hard work. Give your team some time to recognize and celebrate their accomplishments. Acknowledge their efforts, devotion, and commitment to your company's success. Plan company-wide celebrations, team-building exercises, or even meals to express your appreciation and promote a positive work environment. Honoring your team's accomplishments will improve morale and strengthen the relationship between teammates.

12.2.5: Take Advice from Your Accomplishments

Consider your accomplishments and pinpoint the elements that made them possible. Which tactics proved effective? Which choices resulted in success? You can learn a lot from your experiences and obtain insightful knowledge by dissecting your achievements. With this knowledge, you may build your firm and continue to reproduce your successes in the future.

12.2.6 Make New Objectives

It's crucial to keep in mind that your path is not finished, even as you celebrate your accomplishments. Use this chance to establish fresh objectives and ambitions for your company. Think back on your goals and objectives and pinpoint any areas that still require development or expansion. Establish SMART goals—specific, measurable, achievable, relevant, and time-bound—that will inspire and challenge you to keep striving for greater achievement.

12.2.7 Reward others and encourage them

Remember to give back to your community and encourage others to follow their aspirations while you celebrate your accomplishments. Through writing books and articles, speaking engagements, and mentoring programs, you can impart your knowledge and experiences. In addition to fostering the expansion and development of budding entrepreneurs, lending a helping hand to others leaves a legacy that surpasses your personal achievements.

12.2.8 Welcome to on-going development and change.

Success is a journey rather than a destination. Adopt an attitude of constant evolution and progress. Continue to study, be inquisitive, and adjust to the ever-shifting business environment. Seek out fresh chances, investigate creative concepts, and push yourself to achieve greater things. Honor your accomplishments, but never settle for less. Continue moving both your company and yourself forward.

Conclusion (12.2.9)

It's an incredible accomplishment to turn your ideal profession into a profitable business. Honor your accomplishments, be grateful for your experience, and keep developing. It is important to keep in mind that achieving greatness does not always come easily, but it is possible to conquer any hurdle if you have desire, patience, and a clear vision. Continue to dream, to strive, and to celebrate your victories along the way.

12.3 Sustaining Growth and Development

Best wishes! You've been successful in making your ideal career a reality. You've surmounted difficulties, tested your concept, produced a business plan, assembled a working prototype, obtained capital, put successful marketing techniques into practice, assembled a solid team, modified your business plan, expanded your enterprise, controlled risks and difficulties, and preserved a positive work-life balance. Even though you have come a long way, your journey is far from over. We'll look at how you can keep developing as a business owner in this last segment.

12.3.1 Adopting a Growth Perspective

Adopting a growth mindset is vital for entrepreneurs. This entails having an open mind, learning new things all the time, and looking for ways to get better. Being ahead of the curve is crucial since the corporate environment is always changing. Accept change and view it not as a danger but as a chance for personal development. Pay attention to consumer preferences, technology developments, and industry trends. Continue to be inquisitive and flexible in your approach to business so that you can adjust to your clients' evolving needs.

12.3.2 Making an Investment in Ongoing Education

Investing in ongoing learning is crucial if you want to keep developing and changing. To stay current on the newest trends and best practices, attend conferences, workshops, and seminars held by the industry. Join networking and professional associations to meet like-minded people and gain insight from their experiences. To increase your understanding of particular business domains, think about taking online courses or going for advanced degrees. Never forget that information truly is power; the more you know, the more capable you will be to steer your company toward success and make wise judgments.

12.3.3 Getting Input and Assessing Performance

Obtaining feedback from stakeholders, such as employees and customers, is essential for growth and development. Assess your company's performance on a regular basis and pinpoint areas that need work. Survey your customers, get testimonials, and promote candid dialogue among your staff. When making decisions, pay attention to their opinions and consider what they have to say. Utilize key performance indicators (KPIs) to monitor your advancement and assess the efficacy of your tactics. You can find areas for improvement and make data-driven choices by regularly assessing your performance and getting input.

12.3.4 Accepting Originality and Creativity

Creativity and innovation are important forces behind development and evolution. Urge your group to generate creative, original ideas by thinking beyond the box. Encourage a creative culture by offering a secure environment for experimenting and taking chances. Keep abreast of the most recent developments in technology and consider how your company might benefit from them. Accept new business models, procedures, and technology that will help you remain competitive and satisfy changing client demands. You can stand out from the competition and keep improving by embracing innovation and originality.

12.3.5 Reaching a Wider Audience

As your company expands, think about reaching a wider audience. Investigate new regions, focus on untapped clientele, or broaden the range of goods and services you provide. To find unrealized potential and create entry tactics into new markets, conduct market research. To increase your reach, work with strategic partners or think about mergers and acquisitions. You may continue to grow your business and access new revenue streams by reaching a wider audience.

12.3.6 Establishing Powerful Alliances

Creating strategic alliances is one of the most effective ways to expand and change your company. Find complementary companies or groups that have similar goals or ideals to your target market. Work together on joint advertising efforts, cross-promotions, or goods or services that are co-branded. Utilize one another's assets and strengths to forge mutually beneficial alliances. You may expand your brand's reach, get into new markets, and spur growth by forming strategic alliances.

12.3.7 Empowering Others and Giving Back

Remember to inspire others and give back to your community as you develop and progress. Through speaking engagements, mentoring programs, or producing a book similar to this one, you can share your knowledge and experiences. Encourage local nonprofits or causes that share your ideals. Giving back to the community and serving as an inspiration to others not only improves society but also leaves a lasting legacy that extends beyond your company.

12.3.8 Keep dreaming always.

Lastly, keep dreaming of something never-ending. You have demonstrated, as a prosperous business owner, that goals can come true. Keep having big dreams and establishing new objectives for your company and yourself. Push yourself to achieve greater things and change the world. Recall that the path to success is an ongoing process of development and evolution rather than a final destination. Accept the difficulties, acknowledge the accomplishments, and never give up on your dreams.

12.4 Motivating People to Follow Their Dreams

You have surely encountered difficulties, disappointments, and periods of uncertainty on your path from your day job to your ideal career. However, you persisted, and today you may proudly own a prosperous company. Others who might be dreaming of realizing their own ideas can find inspiration in your narrative. Talk to people about your experiences, knowledge gained, and insights. Encourage them to follow their goals, and offer assistance and support when they do so. You can start a positive chain reaction and enable others to write their own success tales by encouraging them to follow their aspirations.

Recall that success is not always simple to achieve, but with perseverance, diligence, and the appropriate attitude, you may make your dream career a reality. So go out, keep developing and growing, and motivate others to follow in your footsteps. More dreamers who are prepared to act and change the world are needed.

12.4 Motivating People to Follow Their Dreams

Best wishes! You've been successful in making your ideal career a reality. You've surmounted difficulties, tested your concept, produced a business plan, assembled a working prototype, secured capital, put successful marketing techniques into practice, assembled a solid team, modified your plan, expanded your enterprise, controlled risks and difficulties, and preserved a positive work-life balance. It's time to encourage people to follow their goals and succeed on their own.

12.4.1 Expressing Your Travel Experience

Sharing your own path with others is one of the most effective ways to encourage others. People enjoy hearing success and triumph stories, especially if they can identify with the difficulties and roadblocks encountered. By talking about your experiences, you can offer insightful commentary and important life lessons that inspire and encourage others to follow their aspirations.

To share your story, think about blogging, doing a TED presentation, or giving a speech at conferences for the industry. Talk openly and honestly about the highs and lows of your experience. Discuss the difficulties you encountered, the errors you made, and the ways in which you overcame them. You may encourage people to persevere and have faith in their own skills by being open and honest about your own difficulties.

12.4.2 Coaching and Mentoring

Taking on the role of coach or mentor is another technique to motivate people. Make use of your experience and skills to mentor and assist budding business owners. Help them deal with the difficulties of launching and expanding a business by giving them guidance, sharing resources, and soliciting feedback.

Think about giving your time to business schools, startup incubators, or local entrepreneurship programs. Organize seminars and workshops or provide one-on-one mentorship. You may expedite others' paths to success and help them avoid common mistakes by sharing your experiences and offering advice.

12.4.3 Networking and Cooperation

In any industry, networking and collaboration are crucial for success. Through fostering partnerships and developing a robust network, you can generate prospects for both yourself and other individuals. Seek opportunities to establish connections with like-minded people, business leaders, and possible partners.

Participate in online networks, join professional organizations, and attend industry conferences. Talk to people, impart your wisdom, and provide a helping hand to those in need. You may both inspire and be inspired by others by establishing connections and promoting a sense of community.

12.4.4 Engaging in Community Service

As your own firm succeeds, it's crucial to return the favor to the community that helped you along the way. Look for opportunities to support causes that share your goals and values. Giving back, whether it be through pro bono work, volunteerism, or charity contributions, can have a significant positive effect on the people you help as well as yourself.

To support prospective entrepreneurs, underprivileged neighborhoods, or social issues, think about forming partnerships with neighborhood organizations or launching your own projects. You can encourage people to follow in your footsteps by leveraging your success to change the world for the better.

12.4.5 Promoting Entrepreneurship

And lastly, promote entrepreneurship. Spread the word about the advantages of following one's aspirations and launching a business by using your platform and influence. Tell success stories, draw attention to how entrepreneurship boosts the economy, and push for laws that help small companies.

To promote entrepreneurship, write articles, give talks at conferences, or participate in public speaking engagements. Raising awareness and encouraging others to take the risk can help foster a culture that values creativity, innovation, and pursuing one's goals.

Recall that encouraging others to follow their goals involves more than just sharing your achievements; it also entails helping and enabling them as they travel their own path. Giving back, mentoring, working together, and speaking up are all ways that you can inspire people and assist them in transforming their ideas into profitable ventures.

Go forward now and encourage people to follow their ambitions!

Finanzas en Pareja: Un Viaje Conjunto hacia el Éxito Financiero

Aitor Moreno Perea